VINTAGE
COMMODORE 128
PERSONAL COMPUTER
HANDBOOK

2019 Survival Edition

BY
MARGARET G. MORABITO
FORMER TECHNICAL MANAGER,
RUN MAGAZINE

ISBN: 9781090260819

Acknowledgment of Registered Trademarks, Tradenames, Service Marks

Photo Credits
Commodore Electronics, Ltd. Cover, #1-1, 1-3, 2-2, 3-5, 3-6, 3-7, 3-9, 3-10, 3-15, 3-16, 3-17, 3-18, 3-19, 5-12, 7-2, 7-3, and 8-2.
Multi-Media Creations #1-1, 2-1, 2-3, 3-1, 3-2, 3-3, 3-4, 3-8, 3-20, 4-2, 5-1, 5-2, 5-3, 5-4, 5-5, 5-6, 5-7, 5-11, 5-13, 5-14 , 6-1, 7-1, 7-6, 8-1, 9-2, 10-1, A-1
RUN Magazine #4-1.
Suzanne Torsheya #5-8, 5-9, 6-3.
Tim Drew #3-12
Margaret Morabito #1-2, 3-11, 3-13, 3-14, 7-4, 7-5

Table of Contents

Foreword by Bil Herd, Commodore 128 Designer

Author's Preface

Acknowledgments

1. Introducing the Commodore 128 Personal Computer   **1**

  1.1 Questions About the Commodore 128   1
  1.2 The C-128 in 2019   8
  1.3 Commodore 128 Specification Chart   16

2. Evaluating a Vintage Personal Computer   **21**

  2.1 Criteria for Evaluating a Vintage Personal Computer   21
  2.2 Commodore International, Ltd.   25
  2.3 The Commodore 128 and Its Competitors   29

3. Looking Closer at the Commodore 128   **39**

  3.1 What Comes with the Commodore 128   39
  3.2 C-64 Peripherals with the Commodore 128   43
  3.3 Getting the Most Out of the Commodore 128   48
  3.4 Other Peripherals for the Commodore 128   66

4. Getting Started   **73**

  4.1 Choosing an Appropriate Work Station   73
  4.2 Setting up the Commodore 128   78

5. Three Computers in One   **83**

  5.1 C-128 Mode   83
  5.2 CP/M Mode   93
  5.3 C-64 Mode   109

6. Productivity with the Commodore 128   **119**

     6.1 Word Processing   119
     6.2 Database Management   123
     6.3 Spreadsheets   126
     6.4 Graphmaking   127
     6.5 Education   129
     6.6 Entertainment   133

7. Telecommunications on the Commodore 128   **137**

     7.1 Introduction to Telecommunications   138
     7.2 Commodore Modems   141
     7.3 Logging into a BBS with a Modem   143
     7.4 Going Online through an Ethernet cable connection   147
     7.5 Going Online through a WiFi connection   153

8. For Programmers   **167**

     8.1 Introduction to BASIC 7.0   168
     8.2 Graphics Capabilities   170
     8.3 Graphics Commands and Statements   173
     8.4 Sprites   179
     8.5 Sound Commands and Statements   184
     8.6 Disk and File Handling Commands   191
     8.7 Programming Aids   196
     8.8 Machine Language Monitor   198
     8.9 8502 Microprocessor Speed Commands   199
     8.10 RAM Expansion Commands   200

9. Software, Disk Images, and More Information   **203**

     9.1 Where to get Software for the C-128   204
     9.2 How to get Software onto the C-128   206
     9.3 How to handle Disk Images   208
     9.4 Where To Look for More C-128 Information   211

10. Maintenance and Service for the Commodore 128   **221**

     10.1 Do-It-Yourself Maintenance   221
     10.2 Service   229
     10.3 Troubleshooting   230

Appendices   **233**

A. Glossary of Computer Terms   233
B. 128 Mode Screen Editing Codes   247
C. CP/M 3 Editing Control Codes and Commands   251
D. 64 Mode Screen Editing Codes   255
E. BASIC 7.0 Glossary   257
F. C-128 Five Configurations   297

Foreword

I think I speak for the entire design team when I say that we did not expect to be discussing the C128 thirty plus year later, let alone that some of the original C128 systems might still be working. I know that I personally would not have thought that there would be a retro-resurgence and a continuing interest in these old machines by people not yet born when the C128 hit the market, but here we are.

I see the phrase "Commodore user" being used once again with new groups springing up in forums and social media thanks in no small part to the availability of the Internet in general and to organizations like the Vintage Computer Federation (VCF). Again this is amazing to me, given the passage of time.

While this book may be coming out 33 years after the C128, its release is timely as more and more users, young and old, look beyond their smart phone and tablet to the time when the seeds of the home computer industry were sown.

It was a time when there were few instruction manuals as to how to do what we did; we were essentially making things up as we went along. We made some mistakes along the way, but I think that Commodore Business Machines mostly got it right and an industry was born with over 27 million Commodore C64s ending up in homes and schools.

To this day I have not worked with a group of people like the team at Commodore where passion and talent were in such abundance, and they remain my extended 8 bit family to this day. The core of the design team, otherwise known as "the animals", was:

Fred Bowen	Terry Ryan	Von Ertwine
Dave Haynie	Frank Palia	Dave DiOrio
Greg Berlin	Dave Siracusa	Terry Fisher

and myself, Bil Herd.
Commodore Senior Design Engineer and C128 Designer

"Link Arms, Don't Make Them"
⟨sys32800, 123, 45, 6⟩

Author's Preface

This is a little piece of Commodore 128 history.

The Commodore 128 Personal Computer Handbook was planned for publication in 1985 and would have been one of the first publications about the newly-released Commodore 128 (C-128). At the time, I was a technical editor for RUN Magazine. In February of 1985, I had a publication contract with DATAMOST, Inc. Researched and written to coincide with the public release of the C-128 in 1985, the book was intended to introduce users to this new computer, based upon information provided to me by Commodore and my first hand experience with an early production version of the C-128. Unfortunately, soon after the manuscript was completed, I was contacted by DATAMOST informing me that they would not be publishing the book. The manuscript sat in a box untouched for nearly 33 years.

Flash forward to 2016. I dug out my C-128 and started using it again, and I started investigating current day usage and support for this computer. Amazing to me and a personal treat was the fact that the C-128 is still very popular worldwide and companies are making hardware and software for it. In early 2018, my son encouraged me to dust off the manuscript and finally publish the book. Thanks to my husband, I was able to find a printout of the original manuscript, the accompanying photos, and the DATAMOST promotional ad. I set out to put it all together again.

As I progressed, I decided to re-focus the book on how to use and enjoy your vintage C-128, keeping as much of the original text as possible. New information has been added specifically aimed at present day C-128 users. As a result, the title of the book was updated to the Vintage Commodore 128 Personal Computer Handbook.

Practical hands-on information is included, such as how to set up the computer, how to access and use the three operating systems, how to set up and use certain modern peripherals, and how to go online with a traditional modem, through the Ethernet, or with a wireless connection. Additional topics include technical specifications, an introduction to BASIC 7.0, maintenance, troubleshooting, repair services, utilizing the C-128 for a variety of applications and entertainment. You will also learn where to look for sources of information on hardware, software, support, and communication with other Commodore computer users. C-64 owners, too, can benefit from this book since many of the new peripherals that work with the C-128 were actually designed for the C-64.

The <u>Vintage Commodore 128 Personal Computer Handbook</u> will be one of your main C-128 reference books, one that you will want to refer back to again and again. Enjoy this book, and more importantly, enjoy your Commodore 128. It still has a lot going for it all these years later...and beyond.

Margaret G. Morabito
January 2019
Rindge, New Hampshire, USA

Acknowledgments

I would like to thank the following people:

Susan West and Fred Bowen of Commodore Business Machines, West Chester, PA, who provided me with information about the Commodore 128 during the early months of research for this book back in 1985.

Commodore Business Machines, for providing me with a Commodore 128 (which I still use today), as well as photographs, promotional materials, and documentation.

Dennis Brisson, the Editor at RUN Magazine, in Peterborough, NH, for his support while I combined my work as Technical Editor for RUN Magazine and did research for this book in 1985.

Bil Herd, who worked for Commodore as a hardware engineer, designed the Commodore 128, and is still active these days in sharing information about this versatile computer. Bil answered a variety of technical questions that I had while updating this book for current day readers.

Mr. Ashley K. Fryer of Black Market Software and Michael A. Morabito, Esq. for proofreading and editing assistance.

Dr. Michael G. Morabito, who was instrumental in getting this book published.

Fig. 1-1. C-128 computer with 1571 disk drive, mouse, MPS 802
printer, 1902 monitor, and 1670 Modem/1200.

Chapter 1

Introducing the Commodore 128 Personal Computer

Let's get started with an informative question and answer session. Included are questions typically asked in 1985, as well as questions from current day vintage C-128 users.

1.1 Questions About the Commodore 128

"I just got a C-128 from a yard sale and I'd like to use it. It didn't come with anything: just the computer. How do I get going?"

Answer: This is a valid question for new owners of the vintage C-128. For help on how to get going, the answer is, "Read this book", and go online with your other computer. Throughout the book, I address new owners, like you. You will learn the easiest ways to get up and running, what to get, where to get it, and where to look for more help.

"What made the Commodore 128 different from other 128K personal computers on the market in 1985, and what makes it a desirable vintage computer today?"

Answer: In 1985, the answer would have been price, performance, and versatility. The C-128 cost less than $300 for its keyboard and CPU. The full 128 system with disk drive and 80-column monochrome monitor cost about $550 ($750 with an 80-column color monitor). Other 128K computers on the market were well over $1,000, and closer to $1,800 with color capabilities. More important, the C-128 came with three built-in operating systems, not one like other personal computers on the market, making it quite versatile and interesting. The C-128 has a Z80 microprocessor which lets the computer run a large number of CP/M business programs. In addition, the C-128 has a built-in C-64 which lets you run the C-64's thousands of software programs and use C-64 peripherals. The C-128 also has a 128K computer built in with the most extensive BASIC ever seen inside a 128K personal computer. The C-128 is memory expandable, up to 640K. Many of the 128K computers on the market back then were limited to 128K.

From the viewpoint of someone trying to decide what vintage computer to get now, many of the reasons that were valid in 1985 are still valid today. The C-128 was the last 8-bit personal computer produced by Commodore, so it is unique in that regard. It has compatibility with the C-64, which still has tremendous support around the world. There are still products being developed that work in 64 and 128 modes, there are users groups and Commodore computer shows, and there is a lot of information and assistance available on the Internet to help you to get the most out of your vintage C-128.

"Can I get onto the Internet with a C-128?"

Answer: Yes. You can get onto the Internet through an Ethernet device or a WiFi modem for your C-128. See Chapter 7 for more details about how to get online and what you can do.

"How much does C-128 software cost and where can I get it?"

Answer: Back in 1985, it varied from program to program, but many software programs used to cost under $50. Some of the more sophisticated ones, like integrated programs, were more expensive. Today, you can buy old software online from sellers on eBay or other online sellers (prices vary), and some of these are pricey. But, you would be wise to simply download software for free from various Commodore sites on the Internet. There are many Commodore web sites and BBSs that provide Commodore programs. See Chapter 9 for more details about where you download free C-128 software.

"I have a 1541 disk drive. Can I use it in the 128 and CP/M modes instead of using the 1571 disk drive from Commodore?"

Answer: Yes. Commodore's engineers built the C-128 so that it could immediately be used by people who already had other Commodore peripherals. The 1541 disk drive that was used with the C-64 will work with the C-128 in all three modes. You will be able to use 128 mode software and the Commodore GCR formatted CP/M software. The drawback to using the 1541 drive is that you will not have the speed and storage capacity found in the 1571 drive, and you won't be able to use commercial CP/M programs.

"Can the C-128 use a tape cassette drive?"

Answer: Yes. You can use the Commodore Datassette tape drive in 128 and 64 modes, but not in CP/M mode.

"What other data storage devices are available for the C-128?"

Answer: In 1985, there was the Commodore 1571 disk drive, which was designed specifically for the C-128. That same year, there was a hard disk drive available from Fiscal Information. Later, there were other disk drives and hard disk drives made for the C-128. Commodore came out with a 3.5 inch floppy drive, the 1581. There is also the 1541 II disk drive. Now, you can get larger capacity devices that will support multi-gigabyte SD cards and USB sticks. See Chapters 3, 5, and 9 for more details.

"Are there fast loaders for the C-128?"

Answer: Yes. You can replace the Kernal ROM with JiffyDOS (from RETRO Innovations). Or, you can get a fast load cartridge. There are also software accelerators.

"Can I use an old non-Commodore monochrome composite monitor for 80-column displays, or do I have to buy an RGBI monitor? What about a flatscreen monitor or TV?"

Answer: You can easily use a monochrome monitor with the C-128. You do not have to use a Commodore RGBI color monitor, and you certainly wouldn't need to buy a color monitor if you intend to use your computer primarily for applications such as word processing, database management, spreadsheets, or 80-column online usage. A simple monochrome monitor will connect to the 9-pin port labeled "RGBI" on the back of your C-128. There are several third party companies selling this particular cable. You can also make your own for only about $4 to $5 in parts.

Nowadays, many people will want to use a flatscreen, LCD monitor or TV with their vintage C-128. This is possible. There are many different configurations, so you will need to do a bit of research into what works with your particular monitor/TV. See Chapter 1.2 and Chapter 3 for more information.

"Which printers can be used with the C-128?"

Answer: This is bit complicated. If you want to, you can buy an old Commodore printer from the 1980s, again from places online like eBay or other Commodore parts sites. Any printer that could work on the C-64 can work on the C-128 with the same cable or interface. This includes not only Commodore's own line of printers, but also dozens of third party printers, such as Epson, Gemini, and more. These parallel and RS232 printers will work on the C-128 as long as you buy an interface that will convert the signal from the computer into a signal that the printer can understand. Printer interfaces for the C-128 used to cost from $50 to $100, depending upon your primary applications and type of printer. A graphics interface tends to cost more than a text and number interface. If you have a more modern printer that has a parallel port, then you can use your C-128 with it, but again you will need to get a parallel interface for the C-128.

"Why did Commodore build in a CP/M operating system rather than IBM PC compatible MS-DOS?"

Answer: In 1985, CP/M had been around much longer than MS-DOS and was extremely popular among small businesses. There was an installed user base of approximately two million systems that were running thousands of CP/M programs. Over 500 computer brands ran CP/M programs. There were not nearly as many IBM PC programs available for the IBM PC, and its few clones, as there were CP/M programs for the many CP/M compatibles. Also, IBM (MS-DOS) software was typically priced much higher than comparable CP/M programs and was the leader in the large business arena where decision makers are not spending their own money on software. CP/M software was very high quality, but since most of it was targeted at the small business and independent professional user, it was priced consistently lower than MS-DOS.

Although CP/M new software introductions had begun to slow down by 1985, the software that was being produced was of the same quality as that for MS-DOS machines. Additionally, much of the existing CP/M software had already been converted to run on MS-DOS machines, so that you could share files. The choice between

4

CP/M and MS-DOS was not a choice of which one was better; it was a choice of availability, cost, and personal preference. Both operating systems had similar command structures and software applications, but CP/M tended to be more accessible, was compatible with more computers, and was a wiser investment for the small business user.

As we now know from history, CP/M was surpassed by MS-DOS and it gradually faded into the dust bin of operating systems. However, if you are a retro fan, you might want to experiment with the CP/M mode of the C-128. The system disks are available online for free, as are some of the more popular applications and games programs.

"Where can I get CP/M software and what kind of CP/M software works on the C-128?"

Answer: You can download CP/M software for free from the Internet or from a Bulletin Board System (BBS). You should try to find Commodore GCR formatted software which is guaranteed to run on your computer. The Perfect Series from Thorn EMI, for example, has three integrated business software programs for the C-128: Perfect Writer, Perfect Calc, and Perfect Filer. But, other CP/M software might work and it's worth a try since it's free to download from most places online. For non-Commodore CP/M 80 software, you should look for software that works on the Osborne, Kaypro, Epson, and other CP/M computers. The CP/M 3 of the C-128 is backward compatible with CP/M 2.2. In the 80s, you could get well-tested public domain programs through CP/M users groups. The First Osborne Group (FOG) was a very popular CP/M users group which had a 5,000 program library. FOG closed in the late 80s. But, there are other users groups that are still active, such as the Toronto PET Users Group, which is still alive and well and sells a CD of software for the C-128, including for CP/M mode.

"Can I use a mouse with the C-128 and does it have a GUI?"

Answer: Yes. You can use a Commodore 1351 mouse. GEOS 64 or 128 (Graphic Environment Operating System) is available for free online. This provides a GUI-based operating system for your C-

128 and can be used with either a joystick or a mouse. If you can't find the 1351 mouse, you could use a PS/2 or USB mouse, with adapters to connect to the C-128. See more details in Chapter 3.

"Where do I go for service if something goes wrong with my computer system?"

Answer: Today, you can find Commodore repair services. The best way to locate these is to do an online search and read the Commodore forums. In the next section and in Chapter 10, I discuss my experience with present day repair service. For historical perspective, early in 1985, Commodore implemented a new national service program which authorized hundreds of local computer and electronic equipment dealers to work on Commodore computers. If something went wrong during the warranty period, you just took your computer to your local authorized repair store and the cost was covered by your warranty. Also, Commodore used to offer a free Customer Service phone line, and if they couldn't help, they would let you know where your local repair service was located.

"How can I be sure that the C-128 won't become a future orphan?"

Answer: This was a valid question in 1985. It is kind of a moot point now that we're looking back in time. In 1985, everything was optimistic for Commodore. The intention was for the C-128 to be the next big 8-bit hit (and it was, but the 8-bit era was coming to an end), following on the success of the incredibly popular C-64. Commodore International was one of the oldest microcomputer companies in existence and had the largest installed user base in the world of any computer manufacturer. Commodore made its own semiconductors and peripherals, and it supported any product for seven years after it was discontinued. They were coming out with new computers all the time, it seemed. Based on surveys back then, the C-128 was expected to be the ultimate 8-bit home and education computer. Of course, Apple gave their computers to schools, a marketing strategy that basically kept Commodore from being the educational leader, which in my opinion, it deserved to be. In addition, the C-128 had something the C-64 never had: added appeal because of its wide ranging business use capabilities of the CP/M mode. Commodore was also quickly moving ahead with the Amiga

6

and MS-DOS compatibles. Despite all of this rosy expectation, Commodore stopped producing the C-128 in 1989 (after selling over 4 million units - a pretty big deal) and went out of business in 1994.

To answer this today, I would say that the C-128 is an orphan (like all of the other 8-bit vintage computers out there), but with a big adoptive family and many friends. People are acquiring C-128s from a wide variety of sources, learning how to use them or re-using them if they already had one; companies are making new peripherals for the C-128 and C-64; and new software (although most is for 64 mode) is being produced.

"Why should I get a Commodore 128 rather than a Commodore Amiga?"

Answer: In 1985, this was a relevant question. The Amiga came out at about the same time as the C-128. It was designed for professional graphic design applications and for multitasking, and it became a popular game computer. It had a faster 16/32-bit microprocessor. When the Amiga was first released, it cost twice what you would pay for a complete C-128 system. Back then, the C-128 was more of a common man's computer, for use in small businesses, as well as for entertainment and education. Being compatible with the popular C-64, the C-128 already had a large amount of software and peripherals to choose from, so combined with the lower cost, this made the C-128 a good choice. As a vintage computer, the C-128 stands out in the 8-bit realm, while the Amiga stands out in the 16/32 bit world.

1.2 The C-128 in 2019

Many computers have come and gone. Few have lasted as long as the C-128 has, as is evidenced by the active user base and sale of hardware and software for the C-128 in 2019. When the C-128 was introduced in 1985, there was a lot of excitement about it and with good reason. But, it would have been difficult to guess that, over 30 years later, there would continue to be C-128 users and that there would be new product development for this computer.

Fig. 1-2. The Author's C-128 with SD2IEC (from The Future Was 8 Bit), Ethernet connection (64NIC+ from RETRO Innovations), and Flatscreen TV (from Sanyo)

Back in the late 80s and 90s, there was new hardware and software development for the C-128, of course. In this section, we will be looking at some of the new products that have been developed for the C-128 in more recent years and old products that are still being produced worldwide. (Many of these same products work with the C-64.) The word "world" is significant because the current user base and product development spans the world. There is a lot of activity in Europe,

Australia, Canada, the United States, and in other countries. My experience has been with European countries and the United States. Since there are so many products, individual developers, and companies, it isn't possible here to cover them all. I think the best way to approach this is to write my own personal story of re-entering the Commodore world. There are many newcomers buying retro computers, and there are a lot of us who are unpacking our C-128s and bringing them back into action. If you have just acquired a C-128, and you don't have any other hardware to go with it, here is some advice on the first things to do.

Data Storage Device

When I first started reactivating my C-128 a couple of years ago, one of the first hardware peripherals that I bought was an SD card reader. This tiny device (about 1.5 by 2.75 inches) can serve as your disk drive, or if you already have a floppy disk drive, it can be used as an additional large-capacity drive. What actually led me to look into this was the fact that when I tried to load my 33-plus-year-old 5 1/4 inch Commodore floppies, they basically were so cruddy that they kept gumming up the heads on my disk drives, making the drives unusable. I would clean the heads, get the drives running (I have both 1541 and 1571 drives), and then promptly would ruin the heads again. So, eventually, I got the message that many of my disks were damaging the drives. Upon closer look, I could see the mold spots on some of the disks. I temporarily gave up on the drives and looked for another solution (I'll get back to the drives later).

After some Internet searching, I found a few Commodore forums which opened my eyes to the current day active user base for the C-128 and the C-64. Through some close reading on Commodore forums, I learned that many Commodore people were using SD card readers, and I got the names of some companies that were producing them. The one that I bought is from the United Kingdom - The Future Was 8 Bit (www.thefuturewas8bit.com; aka TFW8B.com). The SD2IEC is a 1541 floppy disk drive emulation for Commodore computers. This little device holds huge amounts of software, and it allowed me to save programs from my older, functioning disks onto the SD card from my Commodore disk drive.

As an aside, back in the 80s, I used to compile and distribute C-64 educational public domain and shareware software on 5 1/4 inch floppies. Commodore users donated these programs to me when I wrote the Resource Center column in RUN Magazine. I have about seven double-sided disks of educational programs from back in the 80s and it was important for me to archive them onto a more permanent medium. Most of the disks were readable, so the SD card served my archival needs.

There are several companies out there that produce SD2IECs, with varying features. I'm not going to list all of the companies that make these devices. More discussion about SD2IECs is in Chapter 3 with a look at two different versions. Check out some of the Commodore forums, look on YouTube, or do a search; you'll find a variety of reviews and recommendations from real users. Or, if you prefer using a USB stick, that device is also available these days; for example, the Ultimate II+ cartridge has USB ports, from Gideon's Logic in the Netherlands.

Fast Loading

One thing led to another during my re-entry into Commodore usage. Once I got the SD2IEC, then I started to research fast loading options for my C-128. I had read in forum posts about using a combination of a fast loader with an SD2IEC. So, I looked deeper. There are different ways to accomplish this. You could use a software option, or a fast loader cartridge, or an internal chip. I decided to go with an internal option, JiffyDOS for the C-128, from RETRO Innovations (store.go4retro.com). This is a Kernal ROM chip replacement for the C-128, and it's been around for a long time. It was fairly easy to accomplish the chip replacement, and it was well worth the price and time. Plus, it kept my expansion port free for another peripheral that I wanted to get later. Combining JiffyDOS with the SD2IEC made an astonishing change to my system. For one thing, it is fast.

From a software viewpoint, by using the CBM FileBrowser (available on the SD card from TFW8B.com, or from commodore.software/ and other locations online), it is easy to search through a system of directories and subdirectories on the SD card to find and run programs. The CBM FileBrowser is written for a variety of Commodore computers, including the C-128, C-64, and VIC-20.

Getting Onto The Internet

My goals were to get onto the Web, do e-mail, and also to be able to Telnet into Commodore BBSs. I wanted to get away from graphics and revert to text-based online usage. While I still had a couple of Commodore modems for my C-128, and they worked, I didn't want to dial long distance into remote BBSs and tie up my phone line when I knew that there might be an alternate way: namely, going online through an Ethernet connection. Like most people these days, I had an Ethernet cable already in the house, so it made sense to see if I could use my C-128 with that. But, could it be possible for an old technology C-128 to get onto a fast Ethernet connection to the Internet? It seemed maybe just a pipe dream. After some Internet searching and forums reading, I got the good news and found some options. There are Ethernet and WiFi devices for the C-128!

I got the 64NIC+ from RETRO Innovations and, with it, their Commodore diskette of data which held some useful utility programs that would help to get me online. The 64NIC+ connects to the expansion/cartridge port, has an Ethernet port, a reset switch, four toggle switches for various purposes, and extra capabilities for loading up to 16 ROM images. More information about the 64NIC+ and also a wireless modem, WiModem, from CBMStuff.com is located in Chapter 7 Telecommunications.

From a software perspective, I needed to learn what to use from the 64NIC+ utilities diskette. Jim Brain, of RETRO Innovations (www.go4retro.com), was helpful during my learning period. I also relied on the information learned from other C-128 users on Commodore forums, such as Lemon64.com (Sweden) and Commodore.ca (Canada), among others. A particular YouTube video that caught my eye during my initial research was done by Dan Wood of kookytech.net, who demonstrated the 64NIC+ on a C-64. I now use KipperTerm (128 version by Sean Peck) to telnet to a UNIX shell account and from there, I can do e-mail and access the Web using Lynx. The UNIX system that I chose to use is sdf.org. I also telnet into a few Commodore BBSs. ParticlesBBS (telnet://particlesbbs.dyndns.org) has been quite useful to me, for example, when I was getting back into the CP/M mode and needed to transfer files from my SD card to CP/M disks on my 1571. I was able to download the needed utility programs for transferring CP/M files from CBM format into CP/M format, and the sysop gave me some tips. I also learned some valuable tips on using a flatscreen TV as a monitor, and that's what we'll look at next.

Using Flatscreen TV as a Monitor

I have a Commodore 1902 color monitor, which works fine with my C-128, but it's big and heavy, and I wanted to use a smaller footprint monitor, like a flatscreen TV. I did more research and reading on the Commodore forums, YouTube videos, BBSs, and I asked questions.

I found out from my research that there are many different ways of accomplishing what I wanted to do. First, you need to decide if 80-column color is important to you; to me, it wasn't since I would be using 80 columns mainly for telnetting around, accessing text-based online services, and doing some word processing. 40-column color was more important since I use the 64 mode to run games and educational software, mostly when my grandkids visit. It's fun for them.

More importantly, from a technical aspect, I needed to decide upon which type of TV or monitor to get since there are so many different configurations and connections. Does the device have VGA, S-video, HDMI, RCA ports? The forums gave advice from a wide variety of users who were using different flatscreen TVs or monitors with wide ranging connection configurations and various levels of success.

I ended up with a low-cost solution. I got a free Sanyo Vizon (CLT2054) LCD color TV from someone who just wanted to get rid of it. That part was easy. Then, I had to figure out how to connect it to my C-128 so that I would have color in 40 columns and a sharp black and white 80 column display. The TV has an S-video input jack, two audio/video input jacks (AV1 and AV2), an antenna input terminal for cable TV, and 480i/p component video/audio input jacks (AV3). There's more there than I'm using.

For my set-up, I am using two different video/audio cables. My husband and I made an 80-column video cable connected from the RGBI ouput on the C-128 to the Y connector on the TV (AV3). One end of the cable connects to the 9-pin connector on the C-128 and the other end is a standard RCA connector. (You can also buy a cable. See Chapter 7 for more discussion of this.) I also have two commercially made 40-column video cables: one with RCA connectors only and the other with a combination of S-video and RCA. Either one can be used. Or, you could attach a cable from the RF port to the TV antenna connection.

So, I have one monitor that covers all of my needs: it displays 40-column color and 80-column black and white. All I do is change the AV number on the TV to change from 40 to 80, and follow the C-128 mode switching methods (which we'll discuss later). This is just one of many possibilities for a flatscreen TV or monitor on the C-128.

Hardware Repair Man

I have another C-128 computer with a 1571 disk drive, both of which needed some fixing. Again, I went online to my usual sources and looked for someone who had a good reputation and works on Commodore computers. I came upon Ray Carlsen, who is located in the United States. His web site is at personalpages.tds.net/~rcarlsen/. I e-mailed Mr. Carlsen about my C-128 keyboard which had a broken plunger on the Help key. He said that he could fix it, so, with Ray's assistance via e-mail, I removed the keyboard from my C-128, packed it well, and mailed it off to him. Within a couple of weeks, I received it back with the new Help key installed, and Ray had also done a good cleaning of the keyboard while he had it. Quick service at a good price. The shipping cost just about the same as the fixing, since I'm on the East Coast and he's on the West.

Later on, when I finally looked closer at my 1571 and tried to fix it myself unsuccessfully, I contacted Ray again, this time about fixing the broken lever on the drive and getting the drive itself to work properly. He followed up quickly. So, I packed it up well, sent it off, and again, within a couple of weeks, I had my 1571 back home, clean, fixed, and working well. He reminded me to inspect old floppy disks on both sides to see if the disk surfaces are streaked or spotted from contamination of some kind, like a liquid spill (my drive had evidence of a liquid spill). Very worn disks, he said, will have wear lines and that can cause clogs so they should not be used.

In both the issue with the keyboard and with the disk drive, Mr. Carlsen gave me the price for the repair as soon as he received the hardware and had looked it over. This was a positive experience and it is heartening to know that there are quality Commodore repair men out there. There are others; this one is just from my own experience.

Where to get Floppy Disks

After I got my 1571 drive all spiffed up, then I started using it regularly with my main C-128 system. I normally have my SD2IEC configured as drive 8 and my 1571 as drive 9. But, before I could start using the 1571, I needed to buy some new 5 1/4 double-sided, double density floppy disks. Part of the reason for getting these was to be able to experiment more with CP/M mode, for which two 1571 drives are good to use. I found a company, RetroFloppy (out of North Carolina; retrofloppy.com), that sells these new old stock items. I ordered 3M disks. Once I had the new disks, I was pleased to start using my 1571 again.

Commodore User Groups and Shows

Back in the 1980s, there were many Commodore user groups and Commodore was a regular exhibitor at big shows, such as the Consumer Electronics Show (CES). The Toronto PET Users Group (TPUG) was large back in the 80s and held a large annual Commodore show. TPUG is still in existence and there is still an annual World of Commodore show. In 2019, there are user groups out there and there are Commodore and other retro-computer shows which are held worldwide. Some recent vintage and Commodore computer shows include: the Vintage Computer Festival Midwest (and in other regions) and other Vintage Computer Federation sponsored shows; the ECCC Chicago Expo from Illinois; Commodore Vegas Expo (CommVEx); the Commodore Retro eXpo (CRX) in Las Vegas; the Pacific Commodore Expo NW (Seattle, WA); the World of Commodore Expo in Mississauga, Canada. There are others. So, if you want to interact with other Commodore users, see some interesting new C-128/C-64 products and demonstrations, and see other vintage computers, there are events out there to attend.

Remarks

As you can see, there is a lot of development these days of new peripherals that can be used with the C-128 to bring it into the 21st century. And, there are a lot of people with extraordinary levels of expertise who are willing to lend a hand and share information. As well, you will find a lot of C-128 (and 64 mode) software on the Web and also on Commodore BBSs. There is more going on for the C-64, but the C-128 has some good support, too. If you are just getting back into using your C-128, I suggest that you go online with your other computer (Windows, Linux, etc.) and start to find the sources that I mentioned, which will lead you to other resources. You will find sites where you can download programs and then transfer them over to your Commodore system. There is a bit of a learning curve when you first encounter archived files with extensions like D64 or D71, and you will need to decide upon your preferred option for transferring files. We will get into some of this later on in the book. And, there is plenty of assistance for you online. Don't be too timid to ask questions. Commodore users are friendly and ready to offer help.

1.3 Commodore 128 Specification Chart

Keyboard

92 keys (including space bar)
14-key numeric keypad
8 function keys
27 escape key functions
30 control key functions: 64/128

System

CPU and keyboard with separate disk drive.
Built-in BASIC 2.0, BASIC 7.0,
machine language monitor, and sprite editor.

Dimensions

17 inches wide
13 inches deep
2 1/8 inches (at highest point)
6 pounds

Microprocessors:

CP/M Plus Version 3.0 mode: Z80A
128 mode: 8502 (6502/6510 compatible)
64 mode: 8502 (6502/6510 compatible)

Speed:

CP/M mode: 2.04 MHz (up to 4.04)
* averages about 3 MHz
128 mode: 1.02 or 2.04 MHz
64 mode: 1.02 MHz

Fig. 1-3. Commodore 128 Personal Computer

If you search online for C-128 specifications, you will find slightly differing speeds for the two different processors in the C-128. I decided to go to the source, Bil Herd, to ask about this. Bil stated that the speeds are 1.02 and 2.04 for the 64 and 128 modes [8502 processor]. He clarified the speed for the CP/M mode [Z80 processor]: "The Z80 runs on a gated 4Mhz (4.04). It is turned on and off to line up with the DRAM cycle windows. In a strictly Z80 only system, it can be designed that the DRAM is on demand, and a DRAM cycle typically takes 2 clocks (back then). So, sometimes the Z80 hits it just right and it runs as fast as any 4Mhz system. Other times, it just misses the DRAM cycle and has to wait for the next one, so it ends up being closer to a 3Mhz average than a 2Mhz."

RAM Memory	128 mode: 128K 64 mode: 64K CP/M mode: 59K Transient Program Area
ROM	128 mode: 64K (48K + 16K for DOS) 64 mode: 16K
Expansion	128 and CP/M mode: RAM Expansion Module adds up to 512K
Disk Storage	5 1/4" Floppy 1571 disk drive: 350K to 410K formatted
Data Transfer Rate	CP/M mode: 5200 cps 128 mode: 5200 cps 64 mode: 300 cps
Cassette	Yes
Cartridge	Yes
Software Compatibility	CP/M Plus Version 3. CP/M 2.2. All C-64 software
Sound	6581 SID Chip (Sound Interface Device) 3 voices simultaneously (each has 4 waveforms)
Sprites	64/128 modes: 8 Sprites

Resolution	80 columns: 128/CP/M modes: 640 X 200
	40 columns: 128/64/CP/M modes: 320 X 200
	40 columns: 64/128 modes: multicolor; 160 X 200
Colors	16 in all three modes
Video Display	40 column: composite/TV
	8564 VIC-II (Video Interface Chip)
	80 column: monochrome/RGBI color
	8563 VDC (Video Display Controller)
Connectors	User Port
	RGBI Connector
	RF Connector (TV)
	Channel Selector (TV)
	Composite Video (NTSC)
	Serial Port
	Cassette Port
	Expansion Port
	2 Controller Ports
Other	Reset Button; Power Switch and Socket
Operational	128 mode: 40 columns or 80 columns
	64 mode: 40 columns
	CP/M mode: 40 columns or 80 columns

Fig. 2-1. Evaluating a Vintage Personal Computer, C-128

Chapter 2

Evaluating a Vintage Personal Computer

In this chapter, we will look at some of the criteria that should be used in evaluating a vintage personal computer, a history of the Commodore company itself, and the competition that the C-128 had back in 1985. Most of this information was written for the 1985 consumer, but vintage computer buyers can learn from this, too. Modern additions to the text use this font.

2.1 Criteria For Evaluating a Vintage PC

Why do you want this?

Today, maybe you just want an old computer because it seems like a fun idea. Back in 1985, we asked, "What do you hope the computer will do for you?"

If you will be using your computer for entertainment and games, then be sure that it has a good variety of color graphics and sound for high quality game software. For school purposes, you will want color, sound, ease of use, a good quality BASIC, a selection of educational software, and options for adding other programming languages. For the home, you want a flexible and affordable computer.

For small business use, you will want at least 128K of memory, and, if needed, memory expandability. An 80-column display is preferable so that word processing, spreadsheet work, and accounting applications will be easier to handle. You will want some good business software. Of course, there might also be business applications in which graphics and color will be helpful. The option for larger storage space is also desirable for a business computer.

If you are interested in music, you will want the computer to have a decent sound capability, and one which can play polyphonic sounds. A computer with multi-voices which can be programmed, mixed, and output through external speakers will satisfy a musician. Control over music and sound through the BASIC language of the computer is something to consider.

For computer science and programming functions, you will want a computer which has an excellent quality BASIC and one which has enough memory to accommodate other programming languages, such as Cobol, Fortran, and Pascal.

Cost and Availability of Software and Peripherals

A popular vintage computer will have more software and peripherals available for it, both old original ones and more recently developed add-ons. These products should be easy to find and acquire. Popular vintage computers will have present day support from developers and online advice from users. Much software these days will be provided for free online.

Parts and Repair Ability

You need to be able to get parts if something breaks. And, if you don't want to do repairs yourself, you need to know of someone who can fix the computer and peripherals. Of course, in some cases, it might be cheaper to buy another one or get one for free.

User Groups

Another important area to consider is customer support and the installed user base. In 2019, you won't have customer support for the original computer, of course, but you should get a vintage computer that has a good following. Try to locate a vintage computer user group in your area so that you can get recommendations on hardware and software to buy and advice on other computer-related matters.

In the old days, user groups used to provide an incentive to the manufacturer to provide more customer service and support. Back in the 1980s, Commodore kept in contact with its user groups through its approved user group program. You could get advice on how to start your own user group and, if you already had a group, your user group could obtain approval for membership in the Commodore World User Group by contacting the User Group Coordinator at Commodore headquarters in Pennsylvania. Membership entitled your group to access their national online BBS and to receive multiple subscriptions to the Commodore World newsletter. Technical assistance and information was given directly to user groups through group officials, and you had a direct contact at Commodore to whom you could give your comments and suggestions. Commodore also offered marketing assistance for your user group. Posters, articles, and buttons were available for group activities, and your group could have also been asked to participate in pre-market testing of products. Commodore placed such great value on user groups that their User Group Coordinator traveled extensively, visiting local user groups to answer questions and to give out the latest information on what was happening at Commodore.

In 1985, if you didn't have a Commodore user group in your area, you could join user groups that were open to the public over the telecommunications lines. You just had to buy a modem and have a telephone line. CompuServe, for example, had a separate area devoted to Commodore computer users. QuantumLink was Commodore's dedicated network, solely for Commodore users to connect with other Commodore users.

Today, we benefit from the Internet, where you can communicate with enthusiastic vintage Commodore computer users from around the world. And, there are still Commodore user groups that you can join, regardless of your geographical location. Also, YouTube is a great resource for tutorials and reviews of C-128 and C-64 products.

Manufacturer's Reputation

An underlying consideration for anyone buying a computer in the 1980s was the longevity of its manufacturer. The background of a computer company went a long way to giving you a secure feeling that your computer wouldn't become an obsolete item. Back then, competition was ferocious in the computer industry and that weeded out uncompetitive companies. Consumers were able to be a lot more picky in those days and were demanding many more features for their initial investment. Manufacturers *who couldn't compete sufficiently, disappeared. If a computer company had been around for ten years and had survived the shake-outs of the fast changing computer industry in the 80s, then it was likely that it would be around for quite a while longer. Commodore was among this group.*

2.2 Commodore International, Ltd.

A look at Commodore's history is a look at the history of the personal computer. Commodore was one of the first companies to design, produce, and sell a self-contained personal computer. Over the years, it became a leader in the personal, educational, and business computer markets. Let's start at the beginning to see how the company developed, in the light of mid-1980s optimism.

Fig. 2-2. Commodore Logo

In 1958, Jack Tramiel started the Commodore company in Toronto, Canada, to manufacture portable typewriters. Soon after, they began selling adding machines. Commodore later entered the U.S. market, calling itself Commodore Business Machines, Inc.. By 1967, Commodore had firmly established itself as an international business machines company by opening subsidiaries in Japan, Germany, and Switzerland. It also became the first company to sell electronic calculators in North America.

In the early 1970s, Commodore became a major player in the calculator price wars because it had become a vertically integrated component manufacturer. A company is vertically integrated when it makes its own parts for the products it manufactures and sells. This is beneficial because it keeps costs down and also gives the company tighter control over product reliability, quality, and production schedules. A vertically integrated company can quickly and efficiently make modifications to components and can change products in order to meet consumer demands. Vertical integration allowed Commodore to sell its products for much less than the other major calculator companies. From design and engineering through manufacture and marketing, Commodore controlled each step in the process, and continued to do so in its computer business.

Commodore entered the microcomputer field with its KIM-1 in 1975. This was the first single board home/hobbyist microcomputer and used the MOS designed 6502 microprocessor. In 1976, Commodore bought the company that designed the 6502 chip. These chips had become the most widely used microprocessor in home computers and video game machines; they were used not only by Commodore, but also by Apple and Atari.

In 1977, Commodore introduced the first self-contained personal computer, the PET. This was an amazing computer at the time, as it had a complete keyboard, built-in video monitor, built-in tape cassette for program storage, built-in BASIC, upper and lower case letters, and was available to the general public in either 4K or 8K RAM configurations. The PET was of historical significance in the computer industry as it signalled the importance of totally assembled computer systems, rather than kits. It was an instant success because it gave superior value for its price.

By 1979, the Commodore PET was becoming a mainstay in the educational arena. Commodore computers did not take the number one slot in the U.S. educational market because of Apple's strategy of giving away their computers to schools. However, outside of the U.S., Commodore became the leader in the educational field. With the success of the PET, Commodore decided to devote the major part of its business to computers rather than to calculators, and focused its sales strategies on the European market. By 1979, it held 80% of the microcomputer market in Germany and the United Kingdom. It also was among the top three microcomputer companies in the U.S. along with Tandy and Apple.

Commodore released a line of 80-column display business computers in 1980: the CBM 8000 series. This was Commodore's first launch into the business computer market, but at this time, it already had 22 years of experience in business and office machinery. The CBM 8032 had 32K of RAM, a built-in 80-column monochrome display, a highly advanced BASIC (4.0), and it was sold with a high powered one megabyte double disk drive, the 8050. This computer was still being sold in 1985. You could find 8032s in schools and businesses around the world.

In the latter part of 1980, Commodore introduced the VIC-20 home computer. Most people know the VIC-20 as the computer that started the home computer wars. It was a 5K RAM, 20K ROM, color computer, with telecommunications capability, expansion ability, a full typewriter style keyboard, a 22-column display, and function keys. Many VIC-20 owners used their computers for a wide variety of applications in the home and in schools. In the 1981, the Commodore VIC-20 sold over one million units, more than all other computers combined.

Commodore introduced its fourth major computer, the Commodore 64, in 1982. This is the top selling home computer in the world. It has a 40-column display, 64K RAM, telecommunications ability, built-in BASIC with highly advanced sound and color graphics capabilities, and is interfaceable with hundreds of peripherals. Over 6,000 software products were sold for the Commodore 64 by the mid-1980s. By 1984, there were three million C-64s in homes and schools across the world.

In 1983, Commodore introduced its fifth major computer, the B series of business computers. The B128 was a top seller in the European business market. Also, in 1983, Commodore introduced the first transportable color computer, the SX-64. The SX-64 was C-64 compatible, and had a built-in disk drive and a built-in color monitor.

In addition to all of this hardware activity, Commodore created its own software division in order to ensure a good supply of software for its new computers. Furthermore, by late 1983, hundreds of third party software developers were writing programs for the C-64, thereby giving Commodore computers a clear edge over other home computers in the amount and quality of software available to the public.

In 1984, Commodore bought the Amiga Corporation which was in the process of developing a computer based on the Motorola 68000 microprocessor. This personal computer held a 16/32 bit 68000 Motorola microprocessor and was the first in a new line of multi-tasking personal computers. 1984 also brought the introduction of another first, the first home computer to be sold with built-in integrated software. The Plus/4, with its built-in word processor, database manager, spreadsheet, graphics program, and 64K RAM, established a new benchmark for the home computer market.

Commodore continued to produce and sell computers in the U.S. and worldwide. Releases in the mid-80s included a computer that was based on the 16-bit Zilog processor, an IBM compatible, and a UNIX compatible machine, all marketed in Europe. The C-128 was introduced in the U.S. in 1985. The highly touted Amiga personal computer and, believe it or not, an LCD laptop computer were also planned for introduction in the U.S. in 1985. The LCD laptop was not produced, but you can view a video about this interesting computer by Bil Herd at c128.com/commodore-lcd-teardown .

Interestingly, in 2015, there was a C-64 notepad, the C64p, that was developed independently in the United Kingdom. See www.thefuturewas8bit.com for more information.

Commodore's success wasn't due entirely to its own efforts. It welcomed third party manufacturing of compatible peripherals and software. This open policy helped Commodore's computers to thrive because buyers knew that they could get any peripheral they might need, even if it wasn't made by Commodore.

This is snapshot of the Commodore world as it appeared in 1985, when this book was originally written. Unfortunately, by 1994, the company closed due a range of factors. You can read about the history of Commodore in books and on web sites; you can watch a movie about Commodore. Commodore has widespread fame in the vintage computer world and its rise and fall are well-documented.

2.3   The Commodore 128 and Its Competitors

Preliminary advertisements by Commodore targeted the Apple IIc and the IBM PCjr as the C-128's prime competitors. Even though the IBM PCjr had been discontinued, it was one of the few personal computers that might have offered the C-128 any kind of competition. This section, written from 1985 perspective, provides an overview of the competitive landscape at the time, as well as some information for the modern user on which of these computers may appeal to them most. Modern commentary is provided in this font.

Fig. 2-3. A First Look at the Commodore 128

Microprocessors

The microprocessor, the brain of a computer system, dictates how fast and effectively the computer can perform a task. While other computers have only one, the C-128 has three operating systems, powered by two separate microprocessors. Each of the three operating systems (CP/M, 64, and 128) is powerful enough to command its own separate computer system.

First, the C-128 holds a Z80 microprocessor, one of the most powerful 8-bit processors on the market. Found in hundreds of personal and professional computer systems, the Z80 allows the C-128 to run software written for 8-bit CP/M operating systems. Second, the C-128 has a custom 8502 microprocessor, which can function like the 6502 chip in the C-64. The vast majority of software that C-64 owners have will run on the C-128 because of this microprocessor. The 8502 microprocessor also controls the 128 mode of operation, providing 123K of useable RAM, advanced BASIC 7.0 for programming, and superior color and sound capabilities. This microprocessor has already attracted many software developers as it provides great opportunity for highly developed application software.

The Apple IIc was based on the 65C02 chip, another proven microprocessor almost identical to the 6502 chip in the Apple IIe and the C-64. This 8-bit microprocessor handles the IIc's 128K by bank-switching 64K sections of memory, similar to the way the Commodore handles its 128K.

The IBM PCjr runs from the Intel 8088. This 8/16-bit microprocessor accesses all of its 128K at one time, rather than in 64K banks. For some highly complex numeric computations, the PCjr will perform faster than the 8-bit computers. However, for most applications that home computerists are using, the speed of the 8/16-bit processor wouldn't make a noticeable difference.

All three of these computers have highly capable microprocessors, but the three operating systems in the C-128 allow for more versatility from one machine.

Software

The C-128 matches the Apple IIc in the area of software compatibility; both have a huge base of existing programs from which to choose. The Apple IIc's compatibility with existing Apple IIe educational and entertainment software had been its main marketing strength. Apple boasts that thousands of programs written for the smaller memory Apple IIs are available to Apple IIc owners.

Commodore can make the same claim. As of 1985, there are about 6,000 programs that can run on your computer in 64 mode. However, most of these were developed within the two years prior to the release of the C-128, rather than as long as six years for some of the Apple II family.

There were two major differences between the IIc and the C-128 when it came to software compatibility and potential software development in the future. First, the C-128 had a huge amount of existing CP/M software from which to choose. It can read many CP/M formats, including those for Osborne, Kaypro, Epson, and IBM CP/M 86. There are many commercially available CP/M programs which can run on the C-128, and most of these are business-oriented. There are thousands more which were available from public domain sources, such as CP/M user groups. The second major difference is that the C-128 is memory expandable; the IIc is not. The C-128's ability to add an additional 256K or 512K opens up more opportunity for software development and this, of course, provides more applications for you to choose from.

The IBM PCjr is targeted toward a different audience than the IIc and this is reflected in its software offerings. Unlike the IIc's attachment to a student clientelle, the PCjr is targeted at the business user working at home. With its enhanced 128K configuration, the PCjr can run up to 1,000 programs of the IBM PC's business software; with more memory added on, it could run 2,000 of the existing programs. Like the C-128, the PCjr is memory expandable (up to 640K), but to buy just this extra memory, you would end up spending more than you would spend for a C-128 with its 1571 disk drive.

The C-128 provides strong applications for both groups of users, when compared to the Apple IIc and the PCjr: it is well suited for education and business. Software developers are being attracted to the C-128 because of its BASIC 7.0 which includes advanced graphics and sound commands. This computer has strong potential for upward mobility and application growth.

As we know from history, CP/M went into decline and it turned out that most software companies continued to write for the 64 mode since there was such a huge user base there. It made economic sense to write the same software that would run on both

31

the 128 and the 64, and then just put a sticker on the box that said for the 128 or 64. The Apple company continued to provide their computers for free to schools, so many current day 30 or 40-somethings remember using the Apple in school, and running the only memorable Apple game, Oregon Trail. More discussion of software will appear later in the book.

Built-in BASIC

The BASIC 7.0 of the C-128 is the most advanced BASIC language ever built into a personal computer. It offers over 140 commands. The Apple and IBM personal computers don't offer nearly the same power built in as the C-128 does in 128 mode. The IIc's Applesoft BASIC is almost the same as that in the old Apple II computers, and although it does have easy to use graphics commands, you still have to rely on Poke commands to get any music or to tap its double high resolution graphics.

The IBM PCjr has a BASIC which holds advanced commands for sound, graphics, and programming, but you don't get all of them built in. The PCjr's built-in BASIC only allows saving to cassette and doesn't give you access to all of the graphics features. The C-128 comes with the capability to utilize its advanced features; you don't have to buy extras.

Data Storage

Commodore anticipated the concern of computer owners who want speedy transfer of data and large capacity drives, and developed the 1571 fast disk drive, which can take advantage of all three operating systems. In addition to its 64 mode, which emulates the 1541 at 300 cps and 170K storage capacity, the 1571 drive offers faster transfer rates and larger capacities to accommodate both the 128 mode and CP/M mode. In 128 mode, the transfer rate is a maximum of 5200 cps with a storage capacity of 350K; in CP/M mode, 5200 cps with up to 410K storage. Compared to the Commodore drive, the Apple IIc's internal drive has a very small storage capacity: just 143K. This capacity appears to be adequate for the software running on the IIc, but is a definite limitation for more complex business applications. The PCjr has an internal drive with a 360K storage capacity, less than the 410K of the CP/M mode. In addition, IBM did not provide the PCjr with its own second drive option. Both the IIc and the C-128 have easy options for adding their own second drives.

Sound

The C-128 has its own processor for producing sound and 3-voice music. The 6581 SID chip, with its three voices plus white noise, can be programmed, mixed, and output through external speakers. It has ten instruments preprogrammed into its BASIC. Musical keyboards and voice synthesizers have already been developed to take advantage of this chip which was so popular in the C-64. Even more are likely to appear now that there is so much more memory to play with in the C-128. For programmers, accessing this sound is much easier than it was on the C-64 because of the built-in sound commands of BASIC 7.0.

The Apple IIc has just one voice, which can only be heard from a small internal speaker. It is cumbersome to program, requiring Poke commands. There is really no comparison of sound capabilities between the C-128 and the Apple IIc.

The PCjr is more on the level of the C-128 when you look at its sound capabilities. It has three programmable voices, white noise, and output through external speakers, just like the C-128. The value of a computer's sound capabilities, however, lies not only in the number of voices and kind of output; it is also measured by the ease of control over these capabilities and by the presence of software and hardware good enough to take full advantage of these features. It is the latter point which pushes the value of the C-128 beyond that of the PCjr or any other present day personal computer which can offer similar sound capabilities.

Graphics

All three of these computers have high resolution color capabilities, but there are major differences among them when you look at the cost for accessing this color and the ease of controlling it in your own programs.

The C-128 in its 40-column display offers three modes: 16 colors in text mode; 16 colors in high resolution mode with 320 by 200 pixels; and four colors in low resolution multicolor mode with 160 by 200 pixels. In 80-column mode, it offers 16 colors in text mode with 640 by 200 pixel resolution. (The C-128 does have a bit-mapped mode in 80 column display which can handle two colors on one screen. This mode is not controlled through BASIC, but can be accessed through machine language.) The resolution and number of colors offered are strong in relation to other personal computers that do offer color options in 80-column mode. The C-128 has an advantage over many computers in that it also offers eight sprites. The real strength of the C-128's graphics is seen when you look at the number of graphics commands built into BASIC 7.0 that makes programming much easier. BASIC 7.0 holds commands such as Circle, Box, Paint, Draw, Sprite, and about 15 more. These plain English commands make the graphics ability of this computer easily controllable.

In comparison, the IIc has strong graphics capabilities with a low resolution mode of 40 by 48 with 16 colors, a high resolution mode of 280 by 192 pixels with six colors, and a double high resolution mode of 560 by 192 with 16 colors. There are two reasons, however, why most people won't ever use these color graphics features. Applesoft BASIC does not have any commands built in for accessing its double high resolution graphics, so while you can get to this feature, you need to use machine language calls and pokes. Applesoft BASIC also doesn't have as many varied graphics commands as the C-128's BASIC 7.0.

Furthermore, the Apple IIc's 16 colors don't help much when you can't afford a color monitor. The IIc with an RGB color monitor plus the adapter you have to buy to use it costs more than twice what you will pay for a complete Commodore 128 system with color RGBI monitor. Most computer stores don't stock color monitors for the IIc because of their prohibitive cost. The Commodore 1902 RGBI color monitor not only displays the high resolution color graphics of the C-128, it also acts as a high quality 80-column color monitor, and you don't have to buy an extra adapter. The 1902 monitor is selling for less than $300, compared to over $800 for the Apple color monitor and its adapter.

The IBM PCjr has graphics capabilities fairly comparable to the C-128. In its low resolution mode, you get up to 16 colors with 160 by 200 pixels; in medium resolution mode, you get 16 colors with 320 by 200 pixels. In 80-column mode, you have black and white available with 640 by 200 pixels. You may use four colors at this resolution, but must sacrifice 32K of RAM to do this. (The C-128 uses only 16K of RAM for all of its high resolution color graphics.) The PCjr does have extensive BASIC commands for manipulating its high resolution graphics, but you don't get all of them built into the machine: you have to buy a separate BASIC cartridge. Unlike the IIc, the PCjr is often sold with an RGB color monitor to take full advantage of its color features. The C-128 system with an RGBI color monitor, however, costs about half the price of the PCjr with its color system.

Keyboard

The keyboard is the most personal part of any computer. You touch it, you look at it, and through it, you either easily control your computer or have a hard time. The C-128's keyboard has been ergonomically designed for efficient use and is comfortable, functional, and responsive. Commodore put a lot of research into the C-128's keyboard design and paid attention to details.

The C-128 has 92 keys, including a 14-key numeric keypad. The low profile wedge design is slanted to allow freedom of movement across the keyboard with a minimum of effort. Keycaps are molded to fit the fingertips and the "home keys" (F,J, and 5) have little bumps to help touch typists get into position. The numeric keypad aids in doing calculations and data entry. Commodore even gave the keyboard a dull finish to eliminate glare.

The keyboards of these three computers - C-128, Apple IIc, and PCjr - are significantly different. The Apple IIc has only 63 keys; the PJjr has only 62. Neither the IIc nor the PCjr has a numeric keypad to ease data entry on a large scale. The IIc doesn't have programmable function keys, just two Apple keys which are used like control keys in much of its software. The PCjr has 10 function keys which are accessed through two key presses.

The C-128's keyboard outshines its two competitors. The numeric keypad, programmable function keys, 57 control and escape key functions, its 62 keyboard graphics characters, and its ergonomic design are a few illustrations of its intention to attract serious programmers, as well as users with applications such as accounting, data management, financial planning, and word processing.

Ports for Peripherals

For peripherals, the C-128 has eleven ports, including a user port for attaching a modem, an RGBI connector for use with the 80-column monitors, an RF connector which supplies picture and sound to a television set (for use in 40-column mode), a channel selector for television use, a video connector for use with a composite 40-column monitor, a serial port which handles a printer or a disk drive, a cassette port, an expansion/cartridge port for use with cartridge software, two controller ports for joystick, game paddle, light pen, or mouse, a reset button, power switch, and power socket.

The Apple IIc has ports for one joystick/mouse, a modem, a television, monitor, second disk drive, printer/plotter, and a power supply. It doesn't have a cassette port, a cartridge port, a second joystick port, or an RGBI color monitor port.

The PCjr is more comparable to the C-128. It has ports for a joystick/mouse, audio output, a serial printer, cassette recorder, keyboard cable, an RGB color monitor, composite monitor, an internal modem, and an expansion module.

The C-128 and the PCjr have enough add-on ports to satisfy most of anyone's needs, while the IIc falls behind in its peripheral and expansion capabilities. Of equal importance, the price of adding on these peripherals makes a considerable difference among all three of these personal computers. Commodore sells more computers than Apple and IBM combined, and, with its high volume and cost-efficient production, can sell its peripherals for far less than these competitors. In addition, many existing C-64 peripherals are compatible with the C-128.

In summation, the Commodore 128 compares favorably against the IIc and the PCjr when you factor in the large amount of existing software compatible with the C-128 in the areas of business, education, and entertainment; the three separate operating systems; the extensive built-in BASIC; the cost of peripherals and software; and the professionally designed keyboard.

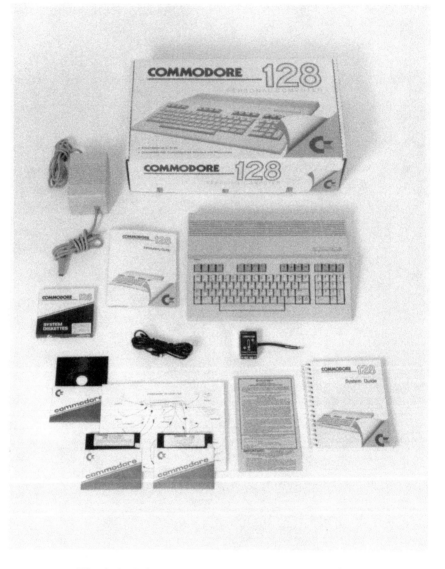

Fig. 3-1. What Comes With the Commodore 128

Chapter 3

Looking Closer at the Commodore 128

The C-128 was designed to be a modular computer system, which is why it is still such a great platform for vintage computer fans. You can build your system piece by piece by adding peripherals as you need them. Most of the material in this chapter is from 1985; however, comments and updates relevant to the present day have been added in this text style.

3.1 What Comes With the Commodore 128

If you are lucky enough to find a complete C-128 system in its original box...

You will find the PC itself, which weighs six pounds and is 17 inches wide, 13 inches deep, and 1/2 to 2 1/8 inches high. The C-128 comes with a heavy duty external power supply, and a cable for connecting the computer to a television. The RF modulator for television compatibility is already built into the computer.

Accompanying the computer are two user's manuals. The Commodore 128 Personal Computer: Introductory Guide (referenced also as the Introductory Guide in this book) is a 35-page manual which leads the new user through the basics of setting up the computer and into the process of loading commercial software. The second manual, The Commodore 128 Personal Computer System Guide (referenced also as the System Guide in this book), is a 404-page manual. It covers a lot of territory and has good introductory sections on how to program in BASIC 7.0.

Two floppy disks are packed with the C-128: the CP/M System Disk with additional CP/M utilities and the Commodore 128 Tutorial and Demo Disk. The CP/M System Disk contains all of the built-in and transient commands needed to handle the CP/M operating system and to run CP/M software. The Commodore 128 Tutorial is a two-hour step by step guide which covers all aspects of the C-128 system. The Demo demonstrates the C-128's graphics and sound capabilities.

You also get a quick reference set-up sheet which illustrates how various peripherals connect to the C-128 and includes the Commodore Hotline telephone number which would have put you in contact with Commodore Customer Service personnel. A warranty card from Commodore was included. By registering with Commodore as a Commodore 128 owner, your computer was covered for three months if anything malfunctioned. (The warranty isn't of much use now.)

If you bought a used C-128, you probably didn't get all of the items originally included. You can still get most of them though. The two user's manuals, the Introductory Guide and the System Guide, are available online in various locations. Commodore.ca has a manuals section, which has the System Guide. Manualslib.com has the Introductory Guide. A quick search on the Internet will also bring up the Programmer's Reference Guide, if you're interested in more advanced programming.

You can download the two disks that came with the C-128 at various locations. You can get the CP/M System Disk and Utilities at www.zimmers.net/anonftp/pub/cbm/demodisks/c128/index.html

or www.cpm8680.com/cpmc64/

These are also provided on the SD card from TheFutureWas8Bit. The C-128 Demo and Tutorial disk is available at commodore.software *and*

www.everythingcommodore.com.

If you need a power supply or a video cable, those are available, too. Ray Carlsen makes new and improved power supplies. Video cables are available from various locations. Many companies and individuals sell Commodore items on eBay.

The Ports

There are 13 ports and switches on the C-128. The expansion/cartridge port is provided for using software cartridges and the RAM memory expansion module. This port opens up the system addresses and data buses to the outside world. It can also be used with special interfaces.

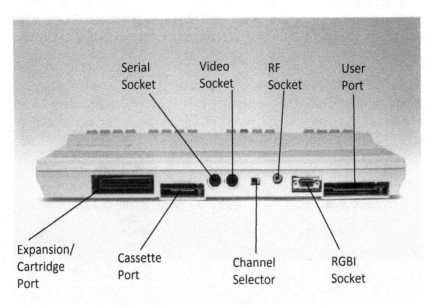

Fig. 3-2. Ports on the back of a C-128

Next, there is a cassette port for the Commodore Datassette, for use with cassette tapes. The Datassette lets you load and save your own programs, as well as run some commercial software in 64 and 128 modes.

A serial port is provided for connecting serial disk drives and serial printers.

There are three video ports. One is for a composite monitor cable which can be used with the Commodore 1702 or other composite monitors. Another is an RF port which is used for connecting the packaged video cable to a television set. A channel selector switch is available for tailoring your computer-television link to your particular area. L is for channel 3 and H is for channel 4 on your television. Be sure to have this switch corresponding with the channel that you have selected on your television. The third video port is for an RGBI monitor. The port has nine pins which put out signals for red, green, blue, intensity, monochrome, horizontal sync, vertical sync, and two grounds. If you already have an 80-column monitor, you can make or buy a cable which will connect your C-128 to your monitor.

A user port is also included on the C-128 which lets you attach peripherals such as a modem or an RS-232 printer interface. On the right side of the computer are two control ports for joysticks, lightpens, graphics tablets, or a mouse.

A reset switch is also built in which will let you restart the computer without turning it off and on again. This reset switch functions in all three modes of operation. An on-off switch and power supply socket are the last of these ports and switches.

With these various connectors, you can add musical keyboards, modems, wireless modems, Ethernet devices, SD and USB devices, graphics equipment, VCRs, and other peripherals to the C-128.

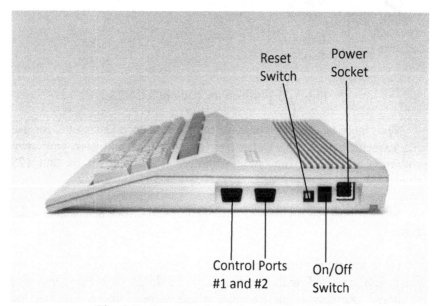

Fig. 3-3. Ports on the right side of a C-128

Since there were so many C-64 owners at the time of the release of the C-128, Commodore made sure that the C-64 peripherals would be compatible. This is great for people today. This section discusses these C-64 peripherals, which are widely available.

Fig. 3-4. C-128 with C-64 Type 1541 Disk Drive

Video Displays

The C-128 has two main video configurations. There are the 40-column display modes that are available in all three operating systems: 128, 64, and CP/M. And, there are 80-column displays in 128 and CP/M modes.

You can use the C-128 out of the box with a black and white or a color television set. Or, you can use the 1701 and 1702 color monitors, both made for the C-64. These monitors will display the high resolution color capabilities in all three 40-column modes. The 1702 color monitor has a 13-inch screen with an NTSC composite signal, with a 40-column

43

by 25-line display. It can display 16 colors with a resolution of 320 by 200 pixels. It has controls for color, tint, brightness, contrast, volume, and vertical and horizontal hold. The sound capabilities of the C-128 are utilized by the built-in audio amplifier and speaker. The 1702 monitor is versatile. It can also display 80 columns in black and white, although it will not be as clear as with an RGB monitor. You attach a cable from the RGBI port on the computer to the front video port on the 1702. Third party manufacturers are making these cables for connecting the C-128 to the 1702, any composite monochrome monitor, and non-Commodore RGB color monitors.

Fig. 3-5. Commodore 1702 Color Monitor

Cartridges

In order to use most computers, you need to buy a disk drive with your initial purchase. The computer won't do much without one. The C-128 was designed with two inexpensive methods of running software and storing data without the need of a disk drive. It is equipped with a cartridge slot. Most people think of a cartridge slot as a means of playing games. True, there are tons of games that can be bought on cartridge for the C-128 in its 64 mode. However, there are education, music, productivity, and business programs available on cartridge, too. (CP/M mode is totally disk-based.) By using a cartridge software program, you don't need to buy any outside peripherals. You just plug the cartridge into the back of your computer, turn on the power, and start computing. One drawback to commercial cartridge software is that you cannot store the results of your computing on the cartridge for future use, but some programs do allow you to save to cassette tape or to disk.

Datassette Storage

When you have to keep track of a larger amount of data, you need some means of permanent storage outside of the computer's memory. The 1530 Datassette unit originally sold for less than $50 and was a good entry level storage device. This tape drive has been used by millions of VIC-20 and C-64 owners during their early experiences with computing. You could get started with the Datassette unit and later advance to a more expensive disk drive. The Datassette will let you save programs that you may have typed in from magazines or that you wrote yourself. There is commercial software available on cassette, too.

Back in 1985, magazines published programs for the C-64 and the C-128. Readers would spend hours typing in these programs and it was a good source of software at the time.

Fig. 3-6. Commodore 1530 Datassette

The most common criticism about tape drives is that they are slow. This is true. You will have to have patience when saving very large programs or files.

45

1541 Disk Drive

The 1541 disk drive is the most widely used peripheral for the C-64. By early 1985, over one and a half million 1541 disk drives had been sold. The 1541 disk drive is well-proven for use in the 64 mode. Many people, however, are not aware that this same drive can be used for utilizing the 128 and the CP/M modes of operation in the C-128.

Fig. 3-7. Commodore 1541 Disk Drive

The 1541 is a 5 1/4 inch floppy disk drive with 170K of data storage. It uses single-sided, single-density disks which can store programs and sequential, relative, random access, and user files. This is a smart drive. It comes with a built-in 6502 microprocessor, two 6522 I/O chips, 2K of RAM, and a disk operating system (DOS) stored permanently in 16K of ROM. This means that the 1541 doesn't have to take up any of the computer's memory to perform its tasks. Many of the disk operations can be performed independently from the computer's processing unit, so the user doesn't have to wait while the drive completes a task. Furthermore, the 1541 can be shared among several computers through the use of a multiuser switch unit.

In addition to the C-64 software that will run on the 1541, software for the 128 mode will work, as long as it only requires single-sided disk access. It is likely that some of the new software for the 128 mode will be designed to run on the 1541 since there are so many 1541s out there already. This makes sense to accommodate the owners of the C-64 drives, making it easier for them to move up to the C-128 for just the price of the computer, and then later buy the newer Commodore C-128 specific disk drives.

As for CP/M, the 1541 will run the new CP/M software being specifically developed for the C-128. This CP/M 3 software adheres to the Commodore GCR format, which is read and write compatible with the 1541. You can also download generic CP/M 3 and CP/M 2.2 programs from bulletin boards and save them onto your 1541 disks.

You should be aware of the limitations of using the 1541 and other C-64 compatible disk drives with the C-128. There are three limitations. First, there is the speed problem. The 1541 transfers data at a much slower pace than the 1571: 300 cps as opposed to up to 5200 cps. If you can put up with the slow pace, then this will not be a big burden immediately; however, knowing that there is a faster and more versatile drive available for your C-128 at a comparable cost to what you paid for your 1541, will probably make you want to get the faster drive. The second limitation is that the 1541 can't read the thousands of off-the-shelf MFM formatted CP/M programs. This means that store-bought programs won't work. Most public domain CP/M software can be used on the 1541 disk drive, as long as it has been received through your modem. The third limitation with using the 1541 is the smaller storage capacity. The 1541 has a capacity of 170K, while the 1571 has up to 410K capacity. (Commodore later came out with another C-64 drive, the 1541-II, which is also compatible with the C-128.)

3.3 Getting The Most Out of the Commodore 128

In this section, we will talk about the Commodore peripherals that were made specifically for the C-128 back in 1985. Using the appropriate 128 peripherals allows you to use all its features. The modular design of the C-128 makes it possible to upgrade peripherals. Today, there are a large number of aftermarket peripherals, allowing people to use SD cards instead of disks, connect to flat screen monitors, and access WiFi! As in other places in this book, text using this font reflects 2019 perspective. Let's look closer at these various items for the C-128...

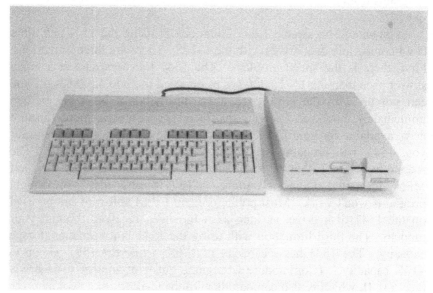

Fig. 3-8. C-128 with 1571 Disk Drive

Monitors

The Commodore 1902 and 1902A RGBI/composite monitors are recommended for use with the C-128. These are dual mode monitors which can be attached to the RGBI port with one connector and to the composite video port with a second connector. You can use two different video cables to connect to the monitor. There also is a single cable which has the two different video outputs from the C-128 spliced into one cable with four RCS monitor inputs on the other end; it has a toggle switch on it so that you can just flip the toggle to change displays. Either cable arrangement will let you take advantage of all of the 40-column color graphics modes in the 64, 128, and CP/M operating systems, as well as the 80-column displays. The 80-column by 25 row display has a resolution of 640 by 200 pixels, one of the highest resolutions available in personal computers today. In the 40-column mode, it duplicates the 1702 composite color monitor, giving you 40 columns by 25 rows with a resolution of 320 by 200 pixels.

The 1902 (pictured below) has a 13-inch screen with controls for brightness, horizontal position, tint, contrast, volume, and 40/80 selection. This monitor is compatible with other computer systems using the RGBI or composite output, and works with videocassette recorders and television tuners. No special cable or interfaces are needed to use this monitor. The 1902A is essentially the same as the 1902. It was released shortly after the 1902 and differs in its cable and switch placement. Both monitors also provide sound.

Fig. 3-9. Commodore 1902 Monitor

You can also use monochrome or RGB/composite monitors from other companies. A monochrome 80-column monitor is good for serious home and business applications, such as word processing, spreadsheet, database, and financial analysis. Many of these monitors can display both 40 and 80 columns by the flick of a switch. If you want to use both displays, you must get two cables: one for the RGBI port which handles the 80-column signal, and one for the composite video port which handles the 40-column signal. If you don't already have a cable to connect to the RGBI port, you can make one by buying a 9-pin subminiature male connector, a phono-video plug, and some microphone cable. Directions for building this can be found on the Internet. You can also buy these cables pre-made.

You can use a TV as your monitor. The C-128 has an RF modulator built in.

More on Monitors

While revising this book, I recently asked Bil Herd (the computer engineer responsible for the C-128) about the video and audio outputs on the C-128. He explained, "The VIC II chip outputs synch, chrominance, and luminance signals and it is the RF modulator, made for us by Mitsumi, that mixed them together to create the RF output as well as the composite video output. In addition, it [VIC-II chip] outputs the separate chroma/luma signals that had better signal to noise aspects and were the favorite of the users with CBM monitors. Since Mitsumi also made the monitor, they tweaked the delays on the signals for best picture and least amount of color edge bleeding. :)"

I also had a question for Bil about the audio output on the C-128 when in 80-column mode. The VDC chip handles the 80-column mode, and if you read the specifications in the System Guide (pg. 352), you will notice that there isn't a pin designated for audio on the RGBI connector diagram. There is an audio pin In and Out for the 40 column video connector. When asked if there is an audio signal from the 80-column mode, he said, "The audio would be the standard SID audio on the Audio out pin of the 40 column DIN. I think most people hooked both 40 and 80 column to the monitor and switched the video source as needed, but the audio stayed on, in either position." So, that explains why you get sound when in 80 column mode.

Flatscreen TV or Monitor

Many people these days will have a newer flatscreen TV or monitor. You can use the C-128 with these flatscreen devices in both 40 and 80 columns. Depending on what you want to do, you can either go with color in 40 columns and black and white in 80 columns; or you can go with color in both screen displays. The possible configurations seem endless and it will all depend on what TV or monitor you have or can get. Your challenge will be to find the particular cable or possibly a video signal conversion device for your particular TV/monitor inputs, which will include ports such as VGA, RCA, or S-Video. The 40 column color mode is easy to figure out. It's the 80-column color display that can get complicated, depending on what TV/monitor you've got. I outlined my particular flatscreen configuration in Chapter 1.2 dealing with this topic. As for cables, there are a variety of outlets where you can buy these. In Europe, there is the Amiga Store (amigastore.eu), for one. In the U.S., I have used 8-Bit Classics (8bitclassics.com). There is a lot of advice about this online in the various Commodore forums, Commodore BBSs, on YouTube, and on individual web sites hosted by Commodore enthusiasts. There are people out there who have built their own devices and cables. It is a deep subject to explore.

Disk Drives

For optimal data storage and file manipulation on the C-128, Commodore developed the 1571 disk drive. The 1571 is a standard 5 1/4 inch floppy disk drive. When formatted, disks can hold 350K of data and up to 410K of data in CP/M mode. For CP/M standard MFM software, either single or double sided, double density formats are useable on the 1571. For 128 and 64 software, both types can be used. A benefit of this drive is not only its large storage capacity, but also its great speed. Its transfer rates are 300 cps in 64 mode, up to 5,200 cps in 128 mode, and 5,200 cps in CP/M mode. Another benefit is the versatility of this drive.

The 1571 has a built-in 6502 microprocessor, 2K RAM, 32K ROM, and its own built-in operating system. It supports most CP/M formats, including IBM CP/M 86. This means that you will be able to use files created on IBM minicomputers. If you have IBM CP/M 86 computers at the office, you could conceivably take those text or data files from work

and use them at home on the C-128. Of course, you would need to have
the same version of the office software in order to read and alter the files.
You can also use Kaypro, Osborne, IBM VER 1, IBM VER 2, and other
CP/M 3 and CP/M 2.2 programs.

The 1571 has two serial ports for daisy chaining, allowing you to
run additional disk drives off the back of your drive. You can also set up
a multiuser system and have several computers accessing the one drive.

Fig. 3-10. Commodore 1571 Disk Drive

*Commodore originally planned to sell a double disk drive for
the C-128. This double disk drive, called the 1572, would have
had the same versatility as the 1571. It was to have a built-in
6502 microprocessor, but with 8K RAM and 64K ROM. (As we
know from history, Commodore never came out with the 1572.
Later, they came out with a 3.5 inch floppy drive, the 1581.)*

If you need even more storage space, there are hard disk drives
available from third party manufacturers. These hard disk drives will

interface with the C-128 through the expansion port. A hard disk drive can hold 10 and 20 megabytes of information and is highly recommended for business and school applications. One company that is working on developing a hard disk drive for the C-128 is Fiscal Information Systems in Daytona Beach, Florida. They already have developed one that works in 64 mode.

There are also fast tape drives that are sold for the C-128. Although these are faster than the Datassette tape drive, you might want to get a faster disk drive, or even a hard disk drive for more productivity from your computer.

If you were around in 1985, the information above was kind of revolutionary for an 8-bit computer. The 1571 was fast and versatile; there was actually a hard disk drive about to come out; and there were fast tape drives. These days, there are a variety of hard disk drives. The most well-known retro company for hard disk drives that we hear about these days is CMD, but in 1985 when I first wrote this book, CMD wasn't in the picture. It was Fiscal Information Systems. Just an interesting tidbit.

"SD2IEC" Data Storage Device

The following information, dealing with SD2IECs, is a newer development in data storage for the C-128. This section is written in 2019.

There are various SD card readers (known also as SD2IEC) for the C-128/C-64. I mentioned some of this back in Chapter 1.1 and 1.2. The SD2IEC allows you to store programs on an SD card and run them on your Commodore. The device connects to the serial port, which is a serial IEEE-488 bus (IEC bus). The serial port is used for connecting disk drives and printers, and in this case, for connecting a 1541 emulator, the SD2IEC.

Mike Murray, of The Geek Pub (www.thegeekpub.com), provides a detailed, easy to understand discussion of the SD2IEC and how it works: "The IEC serial bus is used for many different types of peripherals, the most common two being printers and disk drives...The SD2IEC is a device which emulates the IEC protocol and translates the data being read from and written to an SD card. This allows Commodore computers to read and write to

SD cards rather than to 5.25" floppy disks. A 2GB SD card, for example, can store hundreds of Commodore "D64" disk images and takes up almost no room compared to the Commodore 1541 disk drive and a stack of floppy disks. Additionally, an SD card is far more reliable and less prone to damage compared to floppies." Murray has written and posted an SD2IEC manual on The Geek Pub web site at www.thegeekpub.com/9473/sd2iec-manual-use-sd2iec-c64.

When you acquire an SD2IEC, you will likely be informed that it is upgradable through firmware updates. You might wonder what firmware is. According to techopedia, "Firmware is a software program permanently etched into a hardware device such as a keyboard, hard drive, BIOS, or video card [in our case, an SD2IEC]. It is programmed to give permanent instructions to communicate with other devices and perform functions like basic input/output tasks. Firmware is typically stored in the flash ROM (read only memory) of a hardware device. It can be erased and rewritten" (www.techopedia.com). What this means is that periodically, you can go to the SD2IEC web site (www.sd2iec.de) and update your SD2IEC to get the latest improvements. Ask your SD2IEC dealer for instructions on how to do it. It is pretty simple.

The SD2IEC uses the Commodore disk commands and is compatible with JiffyDOS and other fast loaders. At the time of this writing in 2019, you can find many tutorial and product review videos on YouTube for these devices. Or, look for videos that may have been posted from Commodore shows and conventions.

There are many companies worldwide that produce and sell SD card readers for the C-128. I have worked with the SD2IECs from The Future Was 8 Bit and NC Systems. I have used both in all three operating systems on the C-128: 64, 128, and CP/M (see CP/M discussion in Chapter 5.2 for more details on that). Similar in functionality, these two devices have some differences.

Let's take a look...

"The Future Was 8 Bit" SD Card Interface

The SD card interface from The Future Was 8 Bit was the first peripheral that I bought for my C-128 back in 2016, after having injured a couple of disk drives with aged floppy disks. The SD2IEC is physically small and is shaped like a rectangular box. It is approximately 1 1/2 inches wide by 1 3/4 inches long by 1/2 inch high. It comes in a variety of colors and looks like a tiny 1541 disk drive.

The SD2IEC is powered in various ways. When you purchase it, you select which power source you want. It can be attached to the cassette port or to the user port for power. TFW8B provides an all-in-one cable hard-wired into the device, which has the serial port and power source connectors on it. (I have the cassette port version.) TFW8B also sells an internal version of the SD card interface. And, they offer an external USB-powered SD2IEC, where you use a generic USB power supply (which you buy on your own) for power. Connecting the SD2IEC is simple. In my case, I just connected the device to the serial port and to the cassette port.

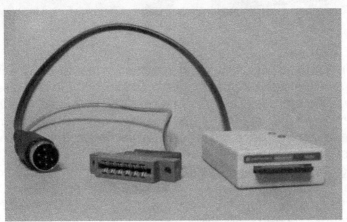

Fig. 3-11. The Future was 8 Bit   SD2IEC
using cassette port power

TFW8B sells an IEC Y-Cable/Splitter/Daisy Chain cable which lets you connect additional serial devices to the C-128, like a Commodore disk drive or a serial printer. The SD2IEC is device

55

#8 by default. This can be changed with a BASIC command. The SD2IEC supports fast loaders such as JiffyDOS, Final Cartridge III, and Epyx Fastload. TFW8B.com also sells the Epyx Fastload Reloaded cartridge. This fast load cartridge is for 64 mode, speeds up the loading of 64 mode software, and includes additional commands for handling the files on your SD card.

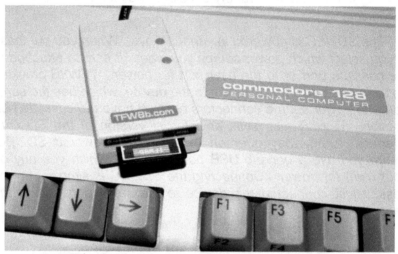

Fig. 3-12.   The Future Was 8-Bit   SD2IEC

There are three buttons on the top of the SD2IEC: Reset, Next, and Previous. Reset moves you back into the root directory of the SD card. Next and Previous buttons are used for running multi-disk image programs, where the original program was designed for two separate disks. When using this device, it is easiest to run the CBM FileBrowser which will let you move among directories and to load and run programs (PRGs) and disk image files (.D64, .D71, .D81). TFW8B sells an 8 GB SD card pre-packed with a variety of C-128, C-64, VIC-20, C-16, and Plus/4 programs and the CBM FileBrowser.

For more information about The Future Was 8 Bit and their SD2IEC, visit thefuturewas8bit.com (or tfw8b.com). You can purchase these through their web site. TFW8B is located in the United Kingdom.

NC Systems Card Reader

The NC Systems SD2IEC card reader is larger, but lightweight. It is 4 inches wide by 5 inches long by 1 1/2 inches high. It comes in a cream color. There is only one way to power the device on your C-128 and that is through the cassette port. Provided with the SD2IEC are two cables. One is a serial cable which attaches to one of the serial ports on the back of the device and to the serial port on the C-128. The other is a cable that connects one end to the cassette port and connects the other end to the back of the SD2IEC.

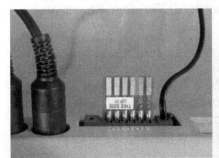 

Fig. 3-13. NC Systems SD2IEC Card Reader (right) and
Cassette Port Pass Through Adapter (left)

The SD2IEC has some valuable features built into it. First, it has two serial ports. One is used for the connection to the C-128 itself and the other can be used to attach an external disk drive or a printer. Additionally, there is a cassette port pass through adapter, allowing you to daisy chain another device off of the cassette port. This is a good feature because you still have the cassette port available for another peripheral even with the SD2IEC connected. For example, you could run a Datassette while also running the SD2IEC. This is handy for copying tape files onto your SD card or vice versa. Another feature is the physical dip switches on the back of the device, which let you change the device number from the default #8. It can be configured to be device 8, 9, 10, or 11 by toggling the switches, just like on a Commodore 1541-II or 1571 disk drive.

Fig. 3-14. Buttons on front of SD2EIC Card Reader

The NC Systems SD2IEC has three buttons on the front with red and green lights, as well as the SD card slot. One of the buttons is a Reset button, resetting back to the root directory of the SD card. The other two buttons are used when handling multi-disk programs. The red light illuminates when saving or for errors; the green light illuminates when loading.

As with other SD card readers, it is best to use a file browser, such as the CBM FileBrowser, to navigate through the directories on the SD card. The SD2IEC handles PRG, D64, D71, D81, and P00 files. It is compatible with GEOS. It supports a variety of fast loaders, such as JiffyDOS, Final 3, Epyx FastLoad, and SJLOAD. Recommended memory card capacity is up to 8 GB.

For more information about NC Systems (formerly RETRO3000) and their SD2IEC, visit their web site at ncsystems.pl. They currently sell through eBay. NC Systems is located in Poland.

Printers

This section gives an overview of the types of printers originally available for the C-128.

Commodore had a line of dot matrix printers - the MPS 802, MPS 803, and MPS 1000 - and the DPS 1101 daisy wheel printer. For C-64 and VIC-20 owners, the earlier 1525, 1526, and 801 printers will work on the C-128. You do not need to buy a separate printer interface to use a Commodore printer. These connect through the serial port, either directly on the C-128, or to the serial port on the back of a disk drive. Third party manufacturers provide many other printers for the C-128 and those may require a separate interface.

A dot matrix printer creates its letters and characters through the combined efforts of many pins that print small dots. The number of dots available in a printer mechanism for creating each character will determine the quality of the print. Some dot matrix printers can create a very high quality of print, close to that of a letter quality printer. Dot matrix printers have a lower print quality than daisy wheel printers (see discussion later), but they have the advantage of being able to print Commodore graphics.

Commodore MPS 802 Dot Matrix Printer

The MPS 802 dot matrix printer gives you close to letter quality print. Termed correspondence quality, the matrix of dots is 8 by 8. This is a bi-directional printer and has the ability to print all upper and lower case letters, all graphics characters, numerals, and symbols. It prints at 60 characters per second, uses a tractor feed, allows 80 character lines of print, and offers true descenders on its letters. The 802 is one of the best dot matrix printers available from Commodore for the C-128.

Fig. 3-15. Commodore MPS 802 Dot Matrix Printer

Commodore MPS 803 Dot Matrix Printer

The MPS 803 is a lower quality dot matrix printer which offers tractor and friction feed options. The 803 will print letters, numerals, and all graphics characters at 60 characters a second. Like the 802, it is bi-directional, offering 80 characters per line. It has a 6 by 7 dot matrix, making this a very good graphics quality printer, but it is not of correspondence quality.

Fig. 3-16. Commodore MPS 803 Dot Matrix Printer

Commodore MPS 1000 Dot Matrix Printer

The MPS 1000 dot matrix printer will print the C-128's high resolution graphics, so you can have hard copies of business charts, graphs, and illustrations. It has bi-directional printing and user-definable characters. The MPS 1000 was designed to be the top of the line dot matrix printer from Commodore.

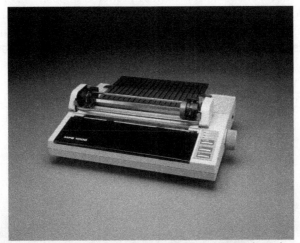

Fig. 3-17. Commodore MPS 1000 Dot Matrix Printer

Commodore DPS 1101 Daisy Wheel Printer

A letter quality daisy wheel printer works differently from a dot matrix printer. Letter quality daisy wheel printers put out clear and crisp letters, numerals, and symbols, but they cannot print high resolution graphics designs. A letter quality printer creates its letters and characters through the use of a daisy wheel which holds the fully formed characters. The daisy wheel rotates until the chosen letter is in position. The letter is then struck by a small hammer which pushes it into an inked ribbon which transfers the character onto the paper. The entire fully formed character is printed so that it looks exactly like that of a good quality typewriter. In fact, a letter quality printer is simply an electronic typewriter without keys.

Fig. 3-18. Commodore DPS 1101 Daisy Wheel Printer

The Commodore DPS 1101 daisy wheel printer prints at a slightly faster rate than most inexpensive daisy wheel printers, 18 cps. It can print from 82 up to 220 characters per line and with proportional spacing. It also has the flexibility of three different pitch settings of 10, 12, or 15 characters per inch. It is a friction feed printer, with a 13 inch maximum width, and it has a Triumph-Adler compatible print wheel.

Many Commodore owners have one of the old Commodore printers or a Commodore-compatible. If you have a printer that has a parallel interface, you can connect that to your C-128 with the addition of a parallel interface.

Modems

On the C-128, you can perform research, business and personal communications, and a wide variety of transactional activities over the telecommunications lines.

For 300 baud telecommunications, you can use the 1660 Modem/300. This auto dial and auto answer modem can be used with touch tone or rotary telephones. It has a built-in speaker so that you can hear your calls being dialed. It also comes with a smart terminal program which will give you access to everything that the online services offer.

Also available is the Commodore 1670 Modem/1200. This modem will give you transfer rates four times faster than the Modem/300 which means that you will spend less time online for data transfer. It utilizes the AT Hayes command protocol, has a built-in speaker, and allows use of either touch tone or rotary dialing. The Modem/1200 offers auto dialing, auto answer, auto baud, auto speed, and auto mode selection. This modem will be used most often by professionals who need to send or receive large data or text files, but anyone who is transferring large public domain software files will also appreciate this fast modem.

For a more detailed look at these two modems and telecommunications on your C-128, see Chapter 7.

Stating that a 1200 baud modem is one that is most often used by professionals sounds a bit odd in the 21st century. But, in 1985, 1200 baud was actually fast. Also, at that time, online activity was still rather limited.

Commodore Mouse

The mouse is an input device which is rapidly becoming widely used in computer software applications. Much software now being written for business applications and home productivity encourages the use of a mouse. The Commodore mouse (1350 and 1351) was developed specifically to take advantage of the new software being developed for the C-128. The mouse controls cursor movement and allows you to choose menu selections without having to type in commands. It also is useful for activities such as painting pictures, since it will duplicate the strokes of a brush.

Fig. 3-19. Commodore Mouse

In 1985, a mouse was still a relatively new device. Most Commodore users had a joystick only, as is the case today. GEOS is probably the most popular mouse-driven software, and there are others. Aside from the Commodore mouse, there is an interface for connecting a PS/2 mouse (Micromys V4) to your C-128/C-64. (PS/2 is a 6-pin mini-DIN connector. Its name comes from the IBM Personal System/2 series of personal computers, introduced in 1987.) There is also the TOM+ adapter for using a USB optical mouse.

Memory Expansion

The C-128's memory can be expanded up to 640 KB through a cartridge known as the RAM Expansion Unit (REU). Commodore sells the 1700 (128KB is added) and the 1750 (512KB is added). A custom controller chip inside the cartridge contains registers that are in the C-128 I/O memory map. This allows the software writer to control data transfers from the added memory by programming those registers. A non-programmer will appreciate the commercial application software that is being written to use this added memory.

There are several BASIC 7.0 commands which let programmers access this expansion memory without using Peeks and Pokes. These commands can transfer a varying length block of data (up to 64K) from any bank of the expansion RAM into any area of the computer's memory or I/O. The opposite can also be performed, as can a combination of the two procedures which will quickly swap a block of data from the C-128 to the expansion module and back.

The additional RAM can also be used in CP/M mode. In this mode, the RAM expansion is treated as a RAM disk for temporary storage of user files. With this expansion, the CP/M operating system can save and load files 200 times faster than the 1571 disk drive.

This expansion module does not require a separate power supply; it runs off of the C-128's own five volt supply.

After 1985, there were other RAM expansion devices that were developed for the C-128. For example, CMD (Creative Micro Designs) came out with the 1750 XL, which went up to 2MB. They also produced RAMLink.

3.4 Other Peripherals for the Commodore 128

Aside from the peripherals and expansion units from Commodore, there are also many third party products. In 1985, the best place to find information on third party peripherals for the C-128 was in magazines devoted to coverage of this computer. These magazines carried advertisements, articles, and reviews of products. Chapter 9 lists these old publications.

Fig. 3-20. C-128 with 1571 Disk Drive, with Zenith Data Systems Monochrome Green Screen Monitor capable of either 80 or 40 column displays

In recent years, some of these magazines have been scanned and are available online for downloading. Commodore.ca has a web page devoted to rare Commodore peripherals and carries some of the original ads. Also, these days, you can read reviews or watch videos about currently produced products online. This list includes what was out there around the time of the release of the C-128. Some of these types of products are familiar and are available today.

Music Synthesizer:

Musical keyboards are available for the C-128. They provide a separate keyboard and can be made to sound like an orchestra, a rock band, a movie soundtrack, or any other type of music and with professional sound quality. You can compose and arrange your own songs and make multi-track recordings on these digital synthesizers.

MIDI Interface:

Musical Instrument Digital Interface (MIDI) is a protocol designed for recording and playing back music on digital synthesizers.

Voice Synthesizer:

These are allophone speech synthesizers which use individual speech sounds strung together to make intelligible speech. Some have a fixed vocabulary, while others can synthesize any word or sentence in the English language. Automatic text to speech conversion from keyboard input is possible in female and male voices.

Video Digitizer:

There are video digitizers which let you transform any item that you can photograph with a video camera into a black and white digital image. These images can be stored on disk and printed out. Digitized images can be changed on screen or combined with text. You can also transfer images via modem to other computers.

Television Tuner for interfacing with monitor:

You can turn your monochrome or color monitor into a television set with a television tuner.

Typewriter-Printer:

Many people buy printers to use with their computers. There was an even more versatile peripheral, the typewriter-printer, which you can use with your C-128. In 1985, the Royal Alpha 620C was one example. This connects to your computer just like any parallel or RS232 printer will, using a low cost interface cable. The benefit, however, is that you would not only get a letter quality printer to use, but you also have an electronic typewriter! For office use, this is more useful than a printer.

We know this didn't catch on, and today it is hard to even find a typewriter in an office!

Multiuser Link:

This will let you network up to eight C-128s together and run them off of one central disk drive. This peripheral is useful for schools and offices where several computers need to share a main data source.

Text Reader:

A text reader will let you input large amounts of data and text into your computer by just sweeping the reader over the page, line by line. One that was advertised in 1985 would read 150 words per minute.

Bar Code Reader:

A bar code reader is used for reading coded information in the form of bars on inventory items. Businesses with large inventories will appreciate the speed and accuracy of a bar code reader.

External Speaker Connector:

You can connect a speaker to your C-128 for use with musical keyboards. and synthesizers.

Cartridge Maker:

This lets a programmer create his/her own software and store it in cartridge form rather than on tape or disk.

Smart Printer Cable:

Many printer interfaces are a combination of a small box and two wires which have to be plugged into both the cassette port and the serial port on the back of the disk drive. There are, however, "smart" cables which require just one connection to your computer. These printer cables run directly off of the serial port on the back of your computer or off the serial port on the back of your disk drive and are much neater.

Serial to Parallel Interface:

Both parallel and IEEE peripherals can be used on the C-128. Interfaces are available which will convert the serial signal from the C-128 into either parallel or IEEE signals.

RS232 Adapter:

The C-128 can use RS232 peripherals. An RS232 adapter or interface is required to accomplish the connection.

Graphics Tablet:

This is one of the more popular drawing peripherals. A graphics input device will let you draw on a flat tablet which transfers your input to the screen. It can also be used for menu selection within software.

Games Paddles:

These are similar to joysticks, as they are used for controlling screen objects.

Light Pen:

Light pens have the ability to interact with software. By placing the light pen near your monitor's screen, you can activate various software options. Used often with graphics programs, the light pen can be a useful peripheral for those people who have difficulty manipulating a keyboard.

Surge Suppressor:

Although this is not always needed, a surge suppressor adds extra insurance to your computer's operation and safety. You won't have to worry about power fluctuations and losing data from your computer's memory if you use this.

Computer Case:

A computer case will let you take your computer with you safely when you are traveling. Many cases are built to accommodate a disk drive also.

Paper Tractor:

This will let you use single sheets of paper in a tractor feed printer.

Computer Covers:

Dust is one of your computer's main enemies. There are various computer covers being sold which will fit any computer.

This ends our look at peripherals.

Fig. 4-1. Commodore 128 Work Station

Chapter 4

Getting Started

The first part of this chapter is historical in nature and is provided here verbatim from the original <u>Commodore 128 Personal Computer Handbook</u>. Readers of Section 4.1 might find this quaint. But, there is some practical advice that you might not have thought about. Section 4.2 is current day information and is needed for setting up your C-128.

4.1 Choosing an Appropriate Work Station

Even before you buy your computer, you should decide upon a location for your work station. A work station is the place where you, your computer, and its peripherals will reside. It is important to consider several conditions when deciding upon the most appropriate location in your home or business for this investment. The following recommendations are not meant to be mandatory, nor is this a complete list. Basically, a comfortable and efficient work station will make you more productive and happier with your computer.

The business user will have to consider who will need access to the computer on a daily basis. The computer should be accessible to the main user so that it can be smoothly incorporated into one's present work routine. If the computer will only be used a few times during the course of a work week, then you could place it in a separate room or in an out of the way spot. However, if someone will be using the computer on a daily basis, it should be placed close by.

Home users should also consider who will be using the computer most of the time, and in addition, who should not have free access to the computer. If you have adults and adolescents in your household who will use the computer, or if you want to encourage these people to learn about computing, then you should select a location which is easy for them to access. There's nothing wrong with setting up your computer in the dining room or family room, as long as it is in a safe location. By choosing a public area within your house, you won't alienate new users who may be reluctant to barge into your private office or your bedroom to try out the computer.

Your main concern in open areas is with the safety of your computer and its peripherals. You don't want your equipment to get banged around, or be subjected to spills and smoke which can damage software, the computer, and its peripherals. You should treat your computer as you would your stereo or television set.

If you have young children who aren't yet at a responsible age, you would be wise to set up your investment in an off-the-beaten-track location such as a study or a bedroom. While you don't want to totally exclude toddlers from playing on the computer, you don't want them to have free access to it when unsupervised.

Another consideration for the home user is time. When will the computer be in use? If someone wants to use it during the day, then any location is fine; but what about what about a teenager who wants to go online at night when the phone rates are lower? You don't want to discourage family members from using the computer by placing it in an awkward location for night time use.

What will your computer be used for? You have a full gamut of applications possibilities for the C-128: education, entertainment, telecommunications, business, family finances, home security, and more. The applications that you and your family members will be using most will dictate the practicality of a proposed location.

If one of your prime activities on the computer will be entertainment, then you probably will want to choose a central location, easily accessible to all. If you intend to use it for educational purposes, then you will want an easily accessible location, too, but one which can be closed off for quiet, undisturbed time on the computer.

If you intend to perform telecommunications activities, you will need a telephone jack close by. This could be as simple as putting in a longer phone cable, or you may have to have an extension phone installed. If your online activities will interfere with normal telephone use, then you might want to put in a separate phone line for your computer area.

If you will be doing a great deal of printing, you should pick a location which will not disturb too many people. Printers are usually loud. A noisy printer can be very disruptive and can prevent someone from hearing a telephone conversation or a television. Many businesses buy hoods for their office printers which deaden the noise. A home user can do the same. If your printer doesn't have to be close by, you can buy a longer cable and place the printer in a separate room.

One often overlooked consideration is the availability of electrical outlets. You will need at least two (depending on your peripherals), and more likely four outlets to carry a basic computer configuration. If you will have a printer, a monitor, a desk lamp, as well as your base computer system unit and a separate disk drive, you're already searching for five outlets or using a power strip.

Try to avoid rigging extension cords. Aside from the hazards of overloaded electrical circuits, it's not worth the risk of lost data from a blown fuse or because someone tripped over the wires and disconnected them. Your equipment should be on a circuit which doesn't have to share current with heavy duty appliances, like a refrigerator or air conditioner, which cycle on and off and cause current fluctuations. If possible, you should have your computer system outlets on a circuit separate from any of those in regular use in other parts of your home or office.

You should have proper lighting wherever you set up your computer. Both glare and insufficient lighting will increase fatigue. Glare on your monitor screen will make your display hard to read. If you see reflections on your screen when your monitor is off, then adjust your lighting or window shades to remove the glare. Your room should be light enough to make it comfortable when you are trying to read manuals, books, numbers from your checkbook or ledger, and other notes.

You should be aware of the room temperature and humidity. Room temperatures should be between 60 and 80 degrees (Fahrenheit). If the temperature goes above or below that range, you won't harm your computer itself as much as you you will harm supplemental materials such as printer ribbons and storage media. High humidity will interfere with electronic connections.

Heat from direct sunlight will damage floppy disks, cassette tapes, and printer ribbons just as it will damage your film when you leave a camera in a hot car. Direct sunlight can also contribute to overheating of disk drives and computers. Aside from the heating effects, direct sunlight can contribute to discoloration of your computer itself, over extended time.

Many people recommend a static free environment for your computer. Take time to assess the situation. If you keep getting little shocks when you touch the monitor or television set, then you should do something about static prevention. Static buildup is usually more of a problem in the dry winter months. If you have a serious static problem, use a rubber mat on the floor or underneath the computer, or spray static guard on the floor. It's not absolutely essential that you take these precautions, as long as you are careful about not zapping your computer with powerful static. If you have three-prong plugs, be sure to use three-hole outlets since the ground connection will help to reduce static.

Another important consideration is space. You should allow yourself and others room to spread out. You may start with only a few disks or tapes and no printer in a neat, little work station, but you will eventually need more room. If you will be doing a lot of word processing, school work, your finances, or your business records, then you will need lots of room. Keep future growth of your work station in mind when selecting a room.

There are several other items to consider. Use a good, comfortable chair, have your keyboard on a desk which is the correct height for efficient typing, and place your monitor so that you don't have to look up or turn your head to see it.

You should also try to select a permanent location. While this is important, in some houses it is not possible. There is less opportunity for damage to your computer system if you are not moving it around frequently. This also helps in keeping track of your disks, tapes, software, books, documentation, telephone numbers, and identification numbers and passwords for online networks.

The underlying advice to keep in mind is to be reasonable. Pick a safe and clean location for your computer system and then make it comfortable. You'll enjoy your computing more. If you know that you like to have a cup of tea or coffee when you work, then provide space for it away from your computer.

Computing does not negate the need for paper, pens, notebooks, and other office supplies., despite what the computer advertisements picture, so leave room for those items in your work area. The computer is just another tool with which you get your work done easier. It doesn't replace all of the traditional study aids, office supplies, and housekeeping records; it adds to them.

Even if this section sounds complicated, it is not. Just use your common sense. If there is an absolute rule about where to put your computer system, it is this: never use the kitchen table. The sight of liquids, food crumbs, cooking smoke, sticky fingers, electrical appliances, and a constant rush of people swirling around is enough to give your computer legs so that it can run to safety.

4.2 Setting up the Commodore 128

Setting up the C-128 is very simple. If you are a VIC-20 or C-64 owner, the procedure is identical to setting up those computers. Be sure that you have decided upon an appropriate location, have plenty of table space, and have at least three outlets available.

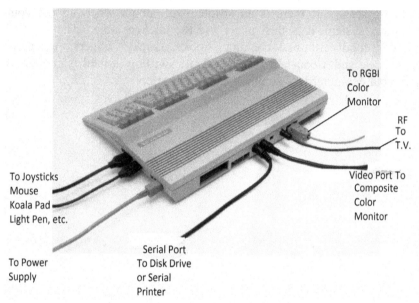

To RGBI
Color
Monitor

RF
To
T.V.

To Joysticks
Mouse
Koala Pad
Light Pen, etc.

Video Port To
Composite
Color
Monitor

Serial Port
To Power   To Disk Drive
Supply   or Serial
                  Printer

Fig. 4-2. Setting up the Commodore 128

Power Supply

The power supply accompanying the C-128 is heavy duty and built for long life. You will notice that it has its own replaceable fuse. The power supply should be placed on a flat, hard surface. Don't place it on a rug or in a dusty location since fibers and dust from these settings can clog up the vent openings and possibly cause overheating of the power supply box.

Always be sure that the power switch on your computer is off before connecting the power supply. Insert the square, 5-pin plug into the port on the right side of your computer labeled "Power". The other end of the power supply's cord will plug into a three-pronged wall socket. You can always keep the power supply attached to the computer. You should unplug the power supply from the wall outlet at the end of the day (or turn off the power strip); there is no need to unplug it after every computing session. The power supply is working even when your computer is off, so don't shorten its life span unnecessarily by always leaving it plugged into an active outlet.

Today, nearly two decades into the 21st century, there are places where you can buy a new C-128 power supply. Mentioned earlier is Ray Carlsen (personalpages.tds.net/~rcarlsen/), who builds C-128 and other Commodore power supplies. Ray builds custom built power supplies that can power several devices at the same time.

Disk Drive

If you are using a disk drive, you will insert the serial cable that comes with your drive into the rear port labeled "serial". The other end of the cable is connected to either of the two serial ports on the rear of the drive. The drive will have its own power cable running to a wall outlet or power strip. If you will be using an additional disk drive, all you have to do is plug its cable into the other serial port on the rear of your first drive. This is called daisy chaining and doesn't require any modifications to your equipment.

If you don't have a 1541, 1541 II, or 1571 disk drive, you can try to buy a used one from the various online outlets, like eBay. But, then you will also need to get software. For a newcomer to the C-128, who just got one from a yard sale or elsewhere without any peripherals, the easiest thing to do would be to get a different storage device, such as the SD2IEC. The SD2IEC plugs into the serial port (and either cassette or user port, for power). It emulates the 1541. There are many companies that produce and sell SD2IECs. You might want to consider getting a fast loading cartridge to go with this. It could be the Epyx FastLoader Reloaded cartridge (from TFW8B.com) or another one that is compatible. TFW8B.com sells the SD2IEC and also sells an SD card that is preloaded with software. These will get you going very well and you'll have more programs than you could normally afford to buy.

Datassette

Just insert the flat cable connector from the Datassette into the back port of the computer labeled "cassette". That's it. The Datassette doesn't require an external power cord. Whenever your computer is on, your Datassette is automatically on as well.

Video Displays

You have three options: composite monitor, television, and RGBI color or monochrome monitor.

If you are using a composite color monitor on your C-128, insert the round 5 or 8-pin plug into the port on the rear of your computer labeled "video". The other ends of the cable are attached to the monitor in either the front or rear connections. You can get a composite video cable from various sources online.

The C-128 has a built-in RF modulator to simplify attaching it to a television set. Simply insert one end of the cable packed inside your computer carton into the rear port labeled "RF". The other end will be attached to the antenna connection on your television set.

Business users will most likely be using either an RGBI color or a monochrome 80-column monitor. Insert the 9-pin plug of the monitor's cable into the rear port labeled "RGBI". The other end is inserted into the monitor.

It is possible for you to have two monitors connected to the C-128 at once. The RGBI monitor can take advantage of the 80-column text displays while the composite monitor displays the color graphics. When using two monitors, you simply connect both cables to the two ports on the computer marked "RGBI" and "video". Both monitors can have displays simultaneously, but only one will receive input at a time.

If you bought your C-128 used and without a monitor, you can just use a TV to get going in 40 column modes. That's the cheapest way since most people have a TV or can get a used one pretty cheaply. You can attach the C-128 to the TV from the RF port directly to your TV RF (antenna/cable) input. The TV's RF (antenna/cable) input will likely be a coaxial connection and might be labeled differently: you will recognize the round, threaded coaxial connector. You don't need the old

Computer-TV box. Get a cable with an RCA plug on one end and a Coaxial screw on or push on connector on the other. This will give you color and sound in the 40-column displays. See Chapter 3 for more discussion about video connections.

Printers

Commodore printers will be connected directly to the port marked "serial". If it is not a Commodore serial printer, it might require an interface. If you already have a disk drive plugged into the serial port, you can plug your printer into the back of the disk drive, which also has a serial port. Instructions for using a particular printer and its interface will be found with those products. If you have any problems, these days, you'll most likely need to go online to find help since you won't be able to find a Commodore dealer for a Commodore printer.

If you got your C-128 used and without any peripherals, I would recommend that you wait on getting a printer. You should try to get the C-128 up and functioning with a data drive of some sort, software, and a video display first. Once you have those set up, get used to the computer. Then, later on, look for a printer, if you really need one. There are many different printers and this is something that will take a while for you to figure out, unless you can get a Commodore serial printer, which would be the easiest option.

Once all of your equipment is connected properly, you are ready to turn on the power. The C-128 will power up in the 128 operating mode. Procedures for powering up in the other two operating modes will be discussed in Chapter 5.

Fig. 5-1. C-128, Three Computers In One

Chapter 5

Three Computers In One

The C-128 was designed to utilize three different operating systems. This chapter will give you a closer look at the three separate modes of operation, and at the keyboard functions on the C-128. You might enjoy working with your C-128 as you read through this chapter. Experiment with the various modes and have some fun. Detailed instructions for moving among all five configurations on the C-128 are given in Appendix F.

5.1   128 Mode

When you first turn on the C-128, it will power up in 128 mode. This gives you 122,365 bytes of free usable RAM for program space, one of the largest amounts of free RAM you will see in a 128K computer. This memory can be expanded up to 640K with a RAM module that you insert into the expansion port. The 128K in this mode is composed of two 64K banks. The lower 64K is for text, and the upper 64K is for storage of variables, arrays, and strings. There is also a 48K operating system in ROM for running BASIC in this mode.

The 128 mode uses the 8564 VIC-II (Video Interface Controller) and the 6581 SID (Sound Interface Device), two separate chips which control the 40-column video output and the sound capabilities. The C-128 also uses the 8563 VDC (Video Display Controller) chip which controls 80-column screen displays. This chip produces the RGBI video output signal which supports text and numeric displays in 16 colors.

How to Access 128 Mode

On powering up, the 128 mode is active. A 40-column display will be in use, unless you depress the 40/80 column key when you turn on the power switch, in which case the 80-column display comes up. If you wish to change from 40 to 80 columns while the computer is running, just press the ESCape key and then press the X key. In order to be able to use both displays, you will need either a dual mode monitor, such as the Commodore 1902, or two separate monitors. You can enter the 128 mode while in CP/M mode by first removing your CP/M disk and then pressing the reset switch on the right side of the computer. You cannot access 128 mode from 64 mode.

The 128 Mode Keyboard

In 128 mode, all of the 92 keys are active, including the numeric keypad. Some of the commonly-used keys are Return, Shift, Shift Lock, Cursor movement, Inst/Del, Run/Stop, Restore, CLR/Home, and the Commodore key. These are detailed in Section 3 of this chapter, dealing with the 64 mode of operation. These keys are used in both 64 and 128 modes. Also, in 128 mode, the C-128 keyboard has 512 individual characters available. These are made possible through two different character sets accessible from the keyboard: 1) upper case letters with two sets of graphics characters, and 2) upper/lower case letters with one set of keyboard graphics characters.

Fig. 5-2. C-128 Two Keyboard Character Sets shown on Front of Keys

Regarding upper case letters with two sets of graphics characters, the keyboard defaults to upper case with graphics mode on powering up. In both 40 and 80 columns, whenever you press an alphabet key, it is in upper case (capitalized). When you press Shift and an alphabet key, the right graphics character on the front of that key will be displayed. Whenever you press the Commodore key and another key, the left graphics character of that key will be displayed.

Regarding upper/lower case letters with one set of keyboard graphics characters, if you are in 40 columns, you can activate the lower case character set by pressing the Commodore and Shift keys together. In this set, all alphabet keys are in lower case, and when shifted, they are capitalized. The left graphics character on the front of the keys will be displayed by pressing the Commodore key and the chosen graphics key. Pressing the Commodore and Shift keys again will exit the lower case character set. You cannot access the right graphics characters in this keyboard set.

If you are in 80-column mode, you activate the lower case set by pressing the Control and N keys together (Ctrl N). By pressing the Commodore key and a key with graphics characters, you will get the left graphics character. You cannot access the right graphics characters in this lower case character set. Pressing RUN/STOP and RESTORE exits the lower case set and it also clears the screen and homes the cursor in the upper left corner.

Fig. 5-3. 128 Mode Command and Control Keys, ESC, TAB, ALT,
CAPS LOCK, CONTROL

The following keys are active in 128 mode:

Escape Key (ESC)

The Escape key in conjunction with other keys can perform 27
functions for screen editing in 128 mode. For example, to create a
window on the screen, you just position the cursor in the upper left
corner of your desired window and press ESC T. Then you position the
cursor on the lower right corner of your desired window and press ESC
B. An invisible screen window is created which will hold subsequent
keyboard entries. By pressing the Home key twice, you can move out of
the window. You may re-enter the window by simply placing the cursor
back inside it, using the normal cursor control keys. Any displays within
the window will remain intact on screen until you either type over them
or clear the screen. The Escape key operations are quite impressive,
giving your C-128 a quality screen editor. Automatic insert mode,
inserting and deleting lines, flashing text, underlining, making a non-
blinking cursor, deactivating screen scrolling, and activating a reversed
screen are just some of the functions that you can control with the Escape
key combinations.

TAB

The TAB key can be used for setting and clearing tab stops on the screen. The function is similar to a tab key on a typewriter. When you press the TAB key, the cursor will move over to your preset stop location. Tabs are preset to 8-column increments in 128 mode. You can erase the tab settings by pressing ESC Z. To reinstate the default 8-column tab settings, press ESC Y. When programming, you can use the PRINT statement with TAB to set your tab settings in a BASIC program.

ALT

The ALT key can be used by programmers to assign a different character set to the keyboard keys. An alternate character set can be programmed and accessed using this key in conjunction with the redefined keys. Unless a specific application redefines a key or a set of keys, pressing the ALT key will do nothing.

CAPS LOCK

The CAPS LOCK key, when in the upper/lower case character set, lets you enter all of the letters in uppercase while still being able to type in numbers and punctuation marks usually accessible only in unshifted mode. On many other computers, when you are typing capital letters, you have to unshift the keyboard in order to access the lower symbols on the keys.

Control Key (CONTROL)

The 128 mode has 18 preprogrammed Control key functions for screen editing. Plus, you also have control over all 16 colors through the use of the Control and Commodore keys used in conjunction with the numbers 1 through 8. The colors are labeled on the fronts of the number keys. See Appendix B for the 128 Mode Control Codes.

Fig. 5-4. 128 Mode Command Keys, HELP, LINE FEED, 40/80
DISPLAY, NO SCROLL

HELP key

A crash occurs when the computer encounters an erroneous
programming statement within a running program. Whenever a program
crashes, or stops unexpectedly, most computers will display some kind of
an error message. This is the same with the C-128; however, by pressing
the HELP key when a crash occurs, you will know exactly where the
error occurred in your program. The faulty line will be displayed on
screen with the precise wrong section of the line highlighted in reverse
video.

LINE FEED

The LINE FEED key advances the cursor to the next lower line on
your screen. The action is similar to the cursor down key and merely
places the cursor directly beneath the current cursor position.

40/80 DISPLAY

The 40/80 DISPLAY key is used to activate the 80-column screen
display. When depressed on powering up, you will enter an 80-column

display as long as you have a monitor attached to the RGBI port. If you don't have a monitor connected to this port, you will simply get a blank screen.

NO SCROLL

The NO SCROLL key stops text from rolling off the top of the screen when you are listing a program or receiving information from an online source. Usually, when the cursor reaches the bottom of the screen, the rest of the lines on screen start moving upward and disappear off the top of the screen. When you press down the NO SCROLL key, the scrolling stops until you have a chance to read what is on your screen. You then reactivate the screen's scrolling by again pressing down the NO SCROLL key, in order to see the rest of the display which is held in memory and ready to be shown on screen.

Fig. 5-5. 128 Mode Cursor Keys

Cursor Keys

The C-128 keyboard has four separate cursor direction keys across the top, each controlling one direction of cursor movement. At the bottom right corner of the keyboard there are two additional cursor keys which each control two directions: the lower arrows show the unshifted direction and the upper arrows show the cursor direction when pressed with the Shift key.

89

Fig. 5-6. 128 Mode Preprogrammed Function Keys and Numeric
Keypad

Function Keys

There are eight function keys on the C-128 which have been
assigned predefined operations to accomplish the activities that are most
frequently used. Pressing a function key eliminates the requirement of
actually typing in a complete command or phrase. F1, F3, F5, and F7 are
accessed by just pressing the key with those labels. F2, F4, F6, and F8
are accessed by pressing the function key in conjunction with the Shift
key.

The predefined purposes of the eight function keys are outlined
below:

F1 GRAPHIC   F2 DLOAD"
F3 DIRECTORY   F4 SCNCLR
F5 DSAVE"   F6 RUN
F7 LIST   F8 MONITOR

The most used function keys are those which will load and run a program (F2 and F6). F3 will display a list of all programs contained on the disk in your drive. F5 will save a program in the computer's memory onto the disk in your drive; you just type in the name of the program after the quotation mark. F7 will list on the screen all of the programming lines of the current BASIC program in memory. F1 will display the Graphic command on the screen. F4 will clear the screen. F8 switches the computer into its machine language monitor for programming in that mode. Exit the M/L monitor by pressing X.

All eight of these function keys can be redefined by you to perform any specific repetitive tasks that you might need. To change their meanings, simply type the command word "Key" to gain access to the definition of these function keys. By typing in a new definition within the quotation marks and pressing Return, you will have redefined your particular function key. When you eventually turn off the computer, these keys lose their customized definitions and revert back to the predefined purposes.

Numeric Keypad

The numeric keypad is active in 128 mode. This eases the job of entering large quantities of numbers when working with accounting applications, when programming many data statements in machine language subroutines, or when simply using the computer as a calculator. The keypad is active in both character sets and in both 40 and 80 columns.

The remaining keys on the 128 keyboard are discussed in Section 3 of this chapter with the 64 mode discussion.

Loading Software in 128 Mode

In 128 mode, you can use disk, cassette, or cartridge software. Usually, only disks and cassettes are used for running your own program creations, those received over modem lines, or those typed out of magazines and books. You won't find much commercial software on cartridge for the 128 mode; however, there are cartridges sold which can be user programmed.

Loading disk-based software can be accomplished in various ways. You could simply press the F2 key, type in the program name, and press the Return key. You could also do it the long way by typing the command DLOAD", then the program name, followed by pressing the Return key. When the blinking cursor appears again, that means that the program has loaded and is ready to activate (run). Type RUN and press Return.

Alternatively, you can take a shortcut on the load and run commands by using RUN with the program name. Type RUN "program name"+Return. This automatically loads and runs the program.

Another method is a carry over from the Commodore 64. Type LOAD "program name",8 (or ,8,1 for a machine language program) and then press the Return key. After a program has loaded into memory, a Ready prompt will tell you that you can now run the program. To run a program, either press F6 or type RUN followed by a Return.

To load a cassette program, type LOAD "program name" and press Return. The screen will prompt you to press PLAY on the cassette recorder. After doing that, just wait for the Ready prompt. Press STOP on the recorder, type RUN, and press Return.

To load a cartridge program, insert the cartridge into the user port before powering up. After the cartridge is in place, then turn on the computer's power. Your program will automatically be activated and appear on screen.

If you are using a modern SD2IEC card reader, use the same loading commands as for a disk drive, or use the automated file browser provided with the SD2IEC.

5.2 CP/M Mode

Commodore included a separate Z80 microprocessor in the C-128, which utilizes the CP/M Plus (aka CP/M 3) operating system. CP/M stands for Control Program for Microcomputers and was developed by Gary Kildall of Digital Research. CP/M Plus Version 3 was designed for computers that had 8-bit microprocessors: the 8080, 8085, Z80 or equivalent. It was the most advanced and the easiest to use CP/M available for 8-bit computers. Using the 128K of RAM built into the C-128, it can also use added memory when a memory expansion cartridge is installed.

Fig. 5-7. CP/M Mode

There were over 500 different business and personal computers which ran CP/M software and over two million CP/M systems being used in the mid-80s. This meant that if you had a CP/M based computer at your job or at your school, no matter what the brand, you would likely be able to share programs with the C-128. You wouldn't have to learn an entirely new set of commands, and you could share files between work and home. If you were a first time computer buyer, the CP/M mode would let you build your software library quickly because there was so much to choose from, including the large amount of public domain software, and because it tended to be less expensive than software made for other personal computers.

By 1979, CP/M was accepted as the standard for 8-bit microcomputer operating systems. It was well-proven and most new 8-bit computers held a microprocessor that ran CP/M. The 8-bit versions of CP/M were known as CP/M 80. There had also been versions made for 16-bit computers (CP/M 86) and for those using the 68000 microprocessor (CP/M 68). Many of the CP/M programs which were developed for CP/M 80 computers were translated for use on CP/M 86 and CP/M 68 computers. The value of the CP/M 80 software was demonstrated by this ability to upgrade onto these faster machines. It also made sharing files between 8-bit and 16-bit CP/M machines possible.

The C-128 can use files made with IBM CP/M 86 software, if you use the 1571 disk drive. If you have an IBM PC that doesn't run CP/M 86, you can buy a utility program that will convert your MS-DOS files into CP/M 86. Then, you can use those files on your C-128. The 1571 disk drive was developed to understand these other different CP/M disk formats. This makes available the use of single-sided, single/double density, and double-sided single/double density disks.

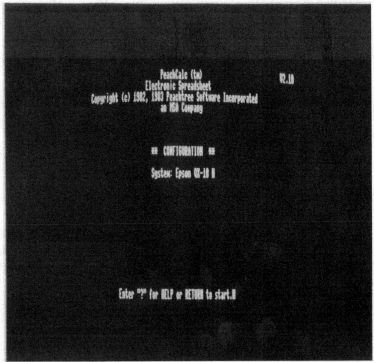

Fig. 5-8. C-128 Running CP/M PeachCalc Spreadsheet Software Made
for Epson Computer

In 1985, there were over 10,000 CP/M programs in existence, many
of which were available for free from user groups and other public
domain sources. Back then, if you wanted to get public domain CP/M
software, you could download it through your modem from a user
group's library or order it on disk by mail from a commercial source for a
small fee. The only drawback to getting public domain software is that
you don't always receive highly detailed documentation, but this became
less of a problem since there were several user groups which published
their own magazines devoted to explaining how to use much of this
public domain software.

How To Access CP/M

There are three methods of booting up CP/M with a disk drive. With the computer off and the drive turned on, place the CP/M system disk into the disk drive; then turn on the C-128. The CP/M operating system will automatically load and execute. If you are already powered up and in 128 mode, you can enter CP/M mode by inserting the CP/M system disk into the drive, typing BOOT, and pressing Return. This will load and activate CP/M mode. The third method for activating CP/M mode is also from within 128 mode. You insert the CP/M system disk into the drive and then press the Reset button.

In order to run a software program in CP/M mode, you simply type the name of the program after the A> prompt on your screen. Press Return and the selected program will automatically load and run. All CP/M sofware is disk-based, as opposed to on tape.

The Commodore 128 Personal Computer System Guide *devotes a chapter to using CP/M mode. This guide is available online at various sites, such as,*

commodore.ca/manuals/128_system_guide/toc.htm

and,

www.zimmers.net/anonftp/pub/cbm/manuals/c128/index.html

For more information, you can download the CP/M Plus Version 3 User's Guide (a reference book was written by Digital Research, Inc., the company that developed CP/M) from the Internet at www.cpm.z80.de/manuals/cpm3-usr.pdf

or at archive.org/details/CPM3-Users-Guide

Fig. 5-9. CP/M 3 System and Transient Commands Directories, 80
columns

CP/M Keyboard and System Disks

In CP/M mode, all 92 keys are active, but some of them perform
different functions than in 128 mode. For example, the eight function
keys are active; however, only F3 and F8 are preprogrammed. F3 will
still give you the disk directory. F8 will display the date of your CP/M
system disk. You can program any key on the keyboard except the Shift
keys, Commodore key, Control, Restore, 40-80 display, and the Caps
Lock key. The numeric keypad works the same as it does in 128 mode.
In CP/M mode, you don't have access to the keyboard graphics designs.

The application software that you run will automatically take
advantage of many of the C-128's keys. When you are not running an
application, you will discover that there are many built-in screen and line
editing features which make programming and handling the screen
display easy.

It is recommended that you use an 80-column display when running
CP/M software because much of the software is formatted for 80
columns. If you are running CP/M on a 40-column display, you will

have to rely on horizontal scrolling to see an entire line, and the applications for which you would be using this could become burdensome and annoying.

New C-128s came with the CP/M System Disk which includes an extensive Help utility as well as the PIP program which you use for making backups of your CP/M disks. On the flip side of the disk is the CP/M System User Utilities Disk. This holds 22 additional files which include Transient commands that the CP/M system uses.

It is likely that you got a used C-128 without the CP/M System and Utilities disks. You can get these online at various web sites. Try, www.cpm8680.com/cpmc64/_ *or*

www.zimmers.net/anonftp/pub/cbm/demodisks/c128/index.html.

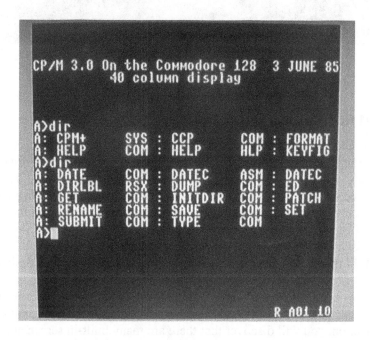

Fig. 5-10. CP/M 3 System and Transient Commands Directories
40 columns

Using CP/M with a Disk Drive

Instructions below are for users who have a disk drive. If you have two drives, that's even better.

One of the first things that you should do when you get your C-128 is backup your CP/M system disk. If you have the 1571, you start by typing HELP COPYSYS at the A> prompt. This will bring up a message telling you that COPYSYS works differently on the C-128 than on other computers. It then proceeds to give you a brief rundown of the steps involved in making a backup CP/M system disk on the C-128.

Here is a summary of what you should do, if you have a single 1571 disk drive, including some helpful hints which the manual doesn't tell you about.

First, insert the CP/M system disk into the drive. Type FORMAT at the A> prompt. This will load into memory the format program which prepares a new disk for use. You will be given three disk types to choose from: C128 double sided, C128 single sided, and C64 single sided. Choose either of the two C128 disk types according to the kind of blank disks that you have.

The screen prompts are easy to follow once you have selected the disk type from the short menu. You will take out the system disk and insert your new disk to be formatted. Press the $ key. Then, wait for it to format. After it has finished, it asks if you want to format another disk. In our example here, type N for no. You will be returned to the A> prompt.

At this point, remove your new disk, place the system disk back inside the drive. Then, type PIP E:=A:CPM+.SYS and press Return. PIP is a system program which will copy files from one disk to another. E is the name of your newly formatted disk. A is the name of the actual 1571 drive which now holds the system disk, which holds the CPM+.SYS program. Punctuation is crucial. Colons and periods must be placed accurately. Don't exchange a comma for a period, or you will get an invalid format message.

When activated, the drive will load the CPM+.SYS program into memory and prompt you to insert Disk E into Drive A. If you aren't familiar with this, you will be wondering what Disk E is. It is your newly formatted disk. After you have done this and pressed Return, the CPM+.SYS program will be copied onto your new disk.

When this is finished, you will be prompted with A>. Then insert Disk A (the original system disk) into the drive. To copy the second program, type PIP E:=A:CCP.COM and press Return. You will be prompted to insert Disk A (the original system disk) in Drive A. You already did this. The drive will load this program into memory and prompt you to insert Disk E into Drive A. Do this. Press Return and the CCP.COM program will be copied onto your new disk.

These two programs, CPM+.SYS and CCP.COM, are the minimum required for making a disk which will boot up CP/M on the C-128.

If you want to make a copy of all of the system disk programs, you can. This is accomplished by typing PIP E:=A:*.* and then following the disk switching prompts. You will be able to copy all the files from one disk to another with this command, but it will take a while because you can copy only one at a time and will be switching disks for each program copy. If you choose to do this, you don't have to bother with first copying the CPM+.SYS and CCP.COM programs. These will automatically be copied using this command.

CP/M on this computer utilizes two 64K banks of memory. The computer can be programmed to activate each 64K bank as required. This lets the operating system reserve one bank entirely for user programs while using the other bank for system operations. There is 59K available for program space.

CP/M Plus has all of the standard CP/M Plus 3.0 commands, but it also has additional features which will make better use of the special capabilities of the C-128. As mentioned before, most of the C-128 keys can be user-defined to generate a specific code or function. In addition, there is an ALT mode which allows the user to send 8-bit codes to a particular application. The default screen for CP/M allows for certain screen controlling features which are achieved on the C-128. Some of these are due to the ADM31 terminal emulation of the C-128's CP/M 3. See Appendix C for a list of the CP/M Control codes and commands.

You can get CP/M software for the C-128, available by downloading from various Internet web sites (see Chapter 9

Software). If you are downloading from the Internet using another computer, there is a bit of a learning curve in transferring those files onto CP/M formatted floppy disks. There are several utility programs for doing the conversion, such as RDCBM (which runs in CP/M mode) and CrossLink (which runs in 128 mode). When I was learning how to do this, I telnetted into a Commodore BBS (particlebbs.dyndns.org:6400) using my C-128, downloaded these CP/M utilities directly onto my 1571 disk drive, and then did the conversions to CP/M mode later.

Another source of CP/M information is the GEnie Commodore group (GEnie was an online service back in the 80s and had a large Commodore following). GEnie has their C-128 files online for downloading, and in there you can find these and other CP/M utilities (www.cbmfiles.com/genie/index.php). The Toronto PET Users Group (www.tpug.ca) sells a CD of Commodore software, including CP/M programs. There is a collection of Infocom games that have been converted into CP/M disk images for the C-128 at www.particles.org/particlesbbs/projects/.

Loading Software in CP/M Mode

Most people who use CP/M are primarily interested in running existing programs rather than writing their own. You don't need to know any commands or screen controlling functions in order to use CP/M software. You must know only the title of the application that you are running.

To run CP/M software, you first boot up the CP/M system. As mentioned earlier, this is done by typing BOOT from the 128 mode and having the CP/M system disk in your drive, or just having the CP/M system disk in your drive when you power up the computer. At the A> prompt, type in the name of the program that you want to run and press Return. (The program name will end with .com, such as zork1.com, but you can omit the .com.) The program will automatically load and run.

2019 Note: Don't confuse the .com CP/M file name with modern day web site domain names.

There are a variety of ways to run CP/M. Aside from running CP/M on a disk drive, some C-128 CP/M users recommend using a hard disk drive or an REU (RAM Expansion Unit).

And, for another option, using an SD2IEC, read the next section.

Using CP/M with SD2IEC (Modern SD Card Interface)

You can run CP/M on an SD2IEC. (This is a device that uses modern SD cards. See Section 3.3) This is good news. This information might save you a lot of research and avoid the necessity of getting a floppy disk drive and learning how to convert files into CP/M format. In my research, I discovered that there are different ways of doing this. I successfully ran CP/M with the SD2IECs from The Future Was 8 Bit and NC Systems. Here are some methods that work for me.

I prefer 80 columns, but you can do this with a 40-column display. I refer to disk images in this discussion. If you are not familiar with those, read Chapter 9.3 and then come back here. If you are using an SD2IEC instead of a floppy disk drive, there is no need to convert the CP/M disk image files as long as they were prepared in the C-128's CP/M mode, but there are still some preliminary steps to do.

Do some preparation first. I call this the "do-before-you-do". Using your other PC, create a directory/folder on your SD card: let's call it "cpm". (Use lower case because the Commodore will display graphics characters instead of upper case letters in the directories.) Inside the "cpm" directory, place your CP/M System Disk image file: I am using "c-128-cpm.system.1987-05-28.d64". To simplify my directory, I rename the files. Ex. Rename "c-128-cpm.system.1987-05-28.d64" to "cpm-1.d64". Also, place into the directory the CP/M Utilities Disk image file - I am using "c128-cpm.utilities.d64" (rename it to "cpm-2.d64") - and an application/game disk image ("zork1.d64" for example). You can find these files online by using the links provided earlier in this chapter.

Download these CP/M disk image files from the Internet onto your SD card using your other PC. That would be the easiest way to get going. After you have done the "do-before-you-do", remove the SD card from your other PC and place it into your SD2IEC on your C-128. Make sure that your SD2IEC is configured as device #8. They normally come as device #8 by default, but just in case you have changed the device number, remember that the SD2IEC must be #8.

You can run CP/M in two ways:

    1) using only the SD2IEC; or

    2) using an SD2IEC and a floppy disk drive.

Let's start with 1).

1) CP/M from an SD2IEC alone

There are two methods when using an SD2IEC by itself without an external disk drive. They depend on whether or not the CP/M disk image file includes the two CP/M system files (CPM+.SYS and CCP.COM).

Throughout this discussion, you will work only from the A> prompt.

a) With System Files included in the disk image:

Using this method is easy, but it might have some limitations in the amount of CP/M software that you can find to use this way. This will only work if the applications/games disk images that you are using were created with the CP/M system files, CPM+.SYS and CCP.COM, included.   The Infocom games collection, for example, has been converted to CP/M for the C-128 by ParticlesBBS sysop, IceBreaker. Each game has the system files included in its disk image.

See www.particles.org/particlesbbs/projects/

In 128 mode, boot up your file browser (such as CBM FileBrowser). Go into your "cpm" directory. From inside the "cpm" directory, using your file browser, highlight your desired application/game, such as "zork1.d64" and press Return. That will say that it's loading and it will hang. Don't worry. Just press the Reset button on your C-128. That will boot up CP/M.

At the A> prompt, type "dir" (or press F3) and you should see the CP/M system files as well as Zork1.com and Zork1.dat. Just type "zork1" and that boots up Zork. Play the game.

This is the easiest method of running applications/games from the SD2IEC on your C-128.

If you only want to get into the CP/M system files, then do the above, but highlight and run the system file disk image (ex. cpm-1.d64) from your file manager. That will boot up just the CP/M system. When you get the A> prompt, you can then type "dir" to see the various files within that directory.

b) Without System Files in the disk image

If you have several CP/M application/game disk images in your "cpm" directory and you want to have the option of running more than one application/game without having to reboot CP/M each time you quit a program, you can do this. It is a bit more difficult. With this, your CP/M applications/games disk images do not require that system files are included in each disk image. This opens up more sources of CP/M programs, such as those from the TPUG collection (referenced earlier; see tpug.ca).

In our example, you should have a "cpm" directory on your SD card and inside that directory, you should have "cpm-1.d64", "cpm-2.d64", "zork1.d64". You can place more than one application/game in this "cpm" directory. For our purposes here, let's add the one more game file: "wishbringer.d71". So, now you have your SD card and your "cpm" directory with four disk image files in it.

Next, you need to do one more preparation. You need to create an "autoswap.lst" file inside your "cpm" directory. Do this on your other PC. Use something like Notepad, and make sure to save it with the "lst" file extension; not "txt" and not as a text file. In the "autoswap.lst" file, you will list all of your disk images, like this:

```
cpm-1. d64
cpm-2. d64
zork1. d64
wishbringer. d71
```

Save the "autoswap.lst" into your "cpm" directory on your SD card. You won't run the Autoswap file; the SD2IEC reads it invisibly.

Put your SD card into your SD2IEC on your C-128 and go into your "cpm" directory.

- *From 128 mode, using CBM FileBrowser, load your "cpm" directory from your SD card.*

- *Find your CP/M Plus System Disk disk image file. In our example, this will be "cpm-1.d64". (It could be a d71 or d81 disk image.)*

- *Press Return to run the disk image, as you would normally do for any other disk image. When you do this, it will display that it is loading, but the system will appear to hang or lock up. Just press the Reset button on your C-128 and watch while your CP/M Plus System boots up.*

- *The A> prompt should display. Type "dir" to get a directory; just so you can see that you actually are in CP/M mode and it's working.*

On the SD2IEC, press the Autoswap button on your device. Depending on which SD2IEC you bought, this might be labeled "next" or maybe there is just one autoswap button, which you should press. When you press the button, you are basically telling the SD2IEC to move into the next disk image file. In our case, we have booted up from "cpm-1.d64". When it reads the Autoswap file, cpm-1.d64 is listed as number one. So, press the "next" Autoswap button twice to move into "cpm-2.d64" which is the Utility Disk. Type "dir" to see where you are.

We want to play the text adventure game, Wishbringer, so press the "next" Autoswap button again to move down into the third entry on your autoswap.lst, which is "zork1.d64". We don't want this one. We want the next one, Wishbringer. So, click the "next" Autoswap button one more time. This should bring you to "wishbringer.d71". To check to make sure this is correct, type "dir" to see the files in that directory. Type "wishbrin" to run the game, Wishbringer. You will notice that in the CP/M directories, the filenames are shortened to eight characters.

If you somehow didn't get into the correct directory, you can press the "previous" or "next" buttons to move through the "cpm" directory until you find what you want. Experiment with it and you'll get the hang of it.

2) CP/M from SD2IEC and a Disk Drive

With this method, you will be working with A> and B> prompts.

In order to run CP/M from an SD2IEC and a floppy drive (I have tested this with a 1571 and 1541), you need to have already prepared a CP/M floppy with some kind of a program on it. For my testing, I put ZORK1 on a Commodore CP/M formatted floppy. You can find ZORK1 online. There is a process for transferring CP/M files from an SD card onto a CP/M formatted disk. You can't just copy them onto a floppy. There is a learning curve and we won't get that part of the process here. (Re-read the section earlier in this chapter dealing with using CP/M with a disk drive. That will help to get you going.)

Configure your SD2IEC as device #8 and your disk drive as device #9. Turn on the disk drive.

- *From 128 mode, using CBM FileBrowser, load a directory from your SD card.*

- *Find your CP/M Plus System Disk disk image file. In our example: cpm-1.d64.*

- *Press Return to run the disk image, as you would normally do for any other disk image. When you do this, it will display that it is loading, but the system will appear to hang or lock up.*

- *Don't worry. Just press the Reset button on your C-128 and watch while your CP/M Plus System boots up.*

- *The A> prompt should display. Type "dir" to get a directory; just so you can see that you actually are in CP/M mode and that it's working.*

Then, type B: to get into the floppy disk. When you have the B> prompt, type "dir" to get a directory. In my case, the directory shows "zork1.dat" and "zork1.com". Type "zork1" and press Return. This will load and run the Zork text adventure game. When finished, type "quit" and that will bring you back to the B> prompt.

Now, you can go back to the SD card by typing A:. If you have another CP/M application or whatever on another floppy, switch floppies now and go back through this process to run your other program. Or, maybe you prepared your CP/M floppy with several programs on it to begin with. That makes it even easier to quit one program and then start up another without leaving the B drive.

Helpful hint: If you happen to be working in black and white, and when you start a CP/M program the screen goes white, you won't see the text because it is also white. Press Control-1 and Return. That should change the text to black so that you can see what you're typing and you can read the screen.

Another tip: If you run into a disk error or want to break out of a program, try Control-C.

So, now you know how to run CP/M Plus (aka CP/M 3) using an SD2IEC. It is fun to work with. There are plenty of CP/M Plus files out there to experiment with. See Chapter 9.1 and 9.4 for more sources of information and software for CP/M.

5.3 64 Mode

The 64 mode of the C-128 duplicates the Commodore 64 computer (C-64). The custom 8502 chip in the C-128 makes C-64 compatibility almost total, because it emulates the original 6510A microprocessor of the C-64. In addition to the compatible microprocessor, the C-128's Sound Interface Device (SID) and the Video Interface Chip (VIC) allow the sound, graphics, and sprite capabilities of the C-64 to be duplicated.

Fig. 5-11. C-64 Mode

In 64 mode, programs or peripherals which could be used on the C-64 can be used on the C-128. There is approximately 64K of RAM and a 40-column by 25 row display. In 64 mode, the operating system resides in 16K of ROM, which includes approximately 8K for Kernal and 8K for BASIC. It includes two character sets, just like the C-64.

The VIC chip displays graphics in 16 colors. Just as in 128 mode, the keyboard graphics are displayed on the front of the keys. These keyboard graphics symbols can be used within programs to create colorful and intricate designs. The 64 mode also offers bit-mapped graphics as well as eight sprites and animation. Sprites, high resolution graphics, and sound are discussed in Chapter 8.

The SID chip gives the computer three independent musical voices, each of which has an eight octave range. Attack, decay, release, and sustain are all controllable. There are also four waveforms: triangle, sawtooth, pulse, and noise, so that you can duplicate specific instruments and create sound effects.

The BASIC 2.0 of the 64 mode allows you to manipulate the sound, graphics, color, and sprites, but not very easily. You have to use Poke and Peek commands. The 128 mode's BASIC 7.0 is much more valuable for programming. If you are interested in graphics, sound, and sprite programming in 64 mode, there are many books available that address these topics in great detail.

How To Access 64 Mode

If you have already powered up in the native mode of the computer, 128 mode, then simply type GO 64, press Return, type "Y" and press Return to switch to the start up message of the 64 mode. Another method of accessing 64 mode is to hold down the Commodore key while powering up.

If you have a C-64 cartridge inserted into the user port, the C-128 will sense the presence of this C-64 cartridge and switch automatically to 64 mode, passing control to the software cartridge.

In order to enter any other mode of operation while in 64 mode, you must turn off the power switch and restart, or press the Reset button. This is because the C-64 doesn't have a command for activating 128 or CP/M modes. Make sure that the 40/80 key is up, since 64 mode works only in 40 columns.

Fig. 5-12. 64 Mode Active Keys (128 mode keys are whited out for illustrative purposes.)

The 64 Mode Keyboard

Not all of the 92 keys of the C-128 are active in 64 mode. The original C-64 computer had only 66 keys. All of these are included on the C-128's keyboard. The other keys do not function in 64 mode.

There are two character sets available in 64 mode, similar to those offered in 128 mode. The graphics characters and the colors can be accessed by pressing Control and/or Commodore keys in conjunction with the desired key. This is the same procedure used on the C-64 and in the 128 mode.

The graphics characters of the keyboard can be changed. All you have to do is to redesign each key to represent a different customized design. This is accomplished through the use of a custom character generator program, many of which are seen in the public domain and in Commodore magazines.

The command keys that are available in 64 mode are the same as those in 128 mode. However, the special keys across the top of the keyboard, such as Escape and Help, are not active in 64 mode. There are also many Control codes which are not active in 64 mode that are active in both 128 and CP/M modes.

Fig. 5-13. Command keys which are active in both 64 and 128 modes. (128 mode keys that do not work in 64 mode have been whited out.)

Let's look at the command keys which are active in both 64 and 128 modes.

CTRL

The Control key is used in conjunction with other keys to perform specific tasks. In addition, the Control key is used in conjunction with numbers 1 through 8 for activating eight of the possible 16 colors. See Appendix D for the list of Control key functions.

RUN/STOP

This key is used to stop the execution of a program. When used with the Shift key, this will automatically load and run a cassette program. In most commercial software and in many machine language programs, the stop function of this key is inactive.

Commodore Key C=

The Commodore key is used almost like the Control key. It can be programmed to perform certain functions when used in conjunction with another key. It is already preprogrammed to display eight colors when pressed in conjunction with the number keys 1 through 8. The

112

Commodore key is also preprogrammed to be used in conjunction with the Shift key. When pressed together, these two keys will toggle between upper case/graphics mode and upper and lower case mode. If you hold down the Commodore key when powering up, you will automatically be placed in 64 mode.

SHIFT

When in the upper and lower case character set, the Shift key is used for capitalizing the letter keys and for accessing the symbols on the tops of the double symbol keys. When in the upper case/graphics character set, the Shift key will access the graphics character on the front right of the keys. In some software, the Shift key will perform a specific function which has been preprogrammed.

SHIFT/LOCK

This key will lock the Shift key so that you will continually access either capital letters or the right graphics designs of the keys.

Fig. 5-14. Command and cursor keys that are active in both 64 and 128 modes. (128 mode keys that do not work in 64 mode have been whited out.)

113

CRSR KEYS

The two cursor keys next to the right side Shift key are used for moving the cursor in four directions. When unshifted, these keys will move the cursor in the direction of the bottom arrows. When shifted, the cursor keys will move the cursor in the direction shown by the top arrows.

CLR/HOME

This is another double function key. When unshifted, pressing this key will place the cursor in the upper left corner of the screen, the home position. When used with the Shift key, this key will erase the entire screen as it repositions the cursor at the home position.

INST/DEL

This key has two purposes. When unshifted, it will delete single characters on screen by moving the cursor one space to the left. When used with the Shift key, it will insert a single space.

RESTORE

The Restore key is used in conjunction with the Run/Stop key. Pressing Run/Stop + Restore, at the same time, breaks out of a running program, clears the screen, and displays the Ready prompt in the home position. To run the program again, type Run and press Return.

RETURN

The Return key is used to enter a line of BASIC into the computer's memory. It will move the cursor to the beginning of the next line. If you press Return when not programming, it will display Syntax Error. The Return key is probably the most frequently used command key on any computer. It is often used in commercial software, for example, to enter the end of a paragraph in a word processor.

Function Keys

The eight function keys are not preprogrammed like they are in 128 mode. They are available in 64 mode, but they must be programmed before they will do anything.

Loading Software in 64 Mode

In 64 mode, you have three different software forms that you can choose from: disk, cassette, and cartridge. All commercial software programs will have loading and running instructions. For loading non-commercial programs, the three procedures are easy to implement.

The C-64 disk-based software requires its own unique syntax. With all of your equipment powered up, your computer in 64 mode, and a disk in the drive, type LOAD "PROGRAM NAME",8 and press the Return key. This will activate the drive and load the particular program named within quotes. For machine language programs, you should type LOAD "PROGRAM NAME",8,1. After a program has finished loading into the computer from disk, the READY prompt will be displayed with a flashing cursor beneath. You must type RUN and press Return to execute the program.

Cassette programs on tape are loaded by first rewinding the tape to the beginning. Then type LOAD "PROGRAM NAME" and press the Return key. The screen will prompt you to PRESS PLAY on the recorder. When you do this, the cassette player will start searching for the specified program and when it locates it on the tape will load it into memory. As with disk loads, the READY prompt will be displayed when the program has completely loaded. You must type RUN and press Return to execute the program. Machine language programs can be loaded from cassette. The syntax for this is LOAD "PROGRAM NAME",1,1.

Cartridges are the easiest to load because there is no command to issue. With the power to your computer off, insert the cartridge into the cartridge (expansion) port and then turn on the computer's power. The software program on the cartridge will automatically load into the computer and start running. You only have to follow the program's prompts. Many commercial programs are sold in sturdy, reliable, and inexpensive cartridges. The drawback to cartridge software programs is that you cannot save and reload files on cartridges.

The data storage medium that you will use most in 64 mode will depend on your purposes. If you are doing a small amount of your own program development in 64 mode and will be typing in programs from magazine sources, you might choose cassette tapes for storage. They are inexpensive and the datassette recorder is one fifth the cost of a disk drive. On the other hand, if you will be doing a lot of programming and will be buying commercially prepared software which will require large file handling such as word processors or database management, you will want a disk drive. The disk drive will let you create and save very large data and text files which can be quickly accessed whenever you need them. Also, most commercial software sold for the C-64 was disk-based.

If you are using a modern SD2IEC card reader, use the same loading commands as for a disk drive, or use the automated file browser provided with the SD2IEC.

This ends our look at the three operating systems of the C-128. Next, we will take a look at productivity applications with the C-128.

Fig. 6-1. Productivity with the Commodore 128

Chapter 6

Productivity with the Commodore 128

This chapter, written in 1985 present-tense, provides some insight into the world that the C-128 entered when it was introduced. Although most of today's users of a vintage computer would not use it for database management or creating graphs for business purposes, this chapter shows that the Commodore company targeted the C-128 to a wide-ranging audience, including businesses, schools, and home users. Their marketing plan was to appeal to all three major groups with this multi-talented 8-bit computer, and productivity was a main purpose for buying the C-128.

Since this chapter is essentially a stroll backwards into history, it has been kept in its original form. It was written for 1985 readers, many who never had a computer before and many who did not even know about these applications. Here we go...

This chapter covers some of the more basic and useful applications that the C-128 can be used for in your business, your home, and in school. There are sections on word processing, database management, and spreadsheet work. Additionally, sections are included on graphmaking, education, and entertainment.

6.1 Word Processing

Word processing is the term used to describe writing and editing text on a computer. A word processor increases productivity by simplifying and speeding up writing tasks. After you write your rough draft, and while it is still on your monitor, you can erase and insert words and paragraphs, correct spelling errors, move text around, and when you are totally satisfied with your product, save it to disk or print it out. Whether you are writing a letter or a book, a word processor is a remarkable tool. It will keep track of your margins, tabs, line spacing, and other formatting requirements. It will store and retrieve often used phrases and paragraphs, and it will keep a permanent record of all of your work. Hardcopies of documents can be printed out in any text style that you choose.

If you now have an electronic typewriter that remembers phrases and paragraphs, you can begin to understand the benefit of a word processor. Take that memory that you have in your typewriter and multiply it 100 times. That's one way to envision the value of a word processor.

What happens when your business has an electrical power failure? All of your electronic typewriters lose their memories. This is a permanent loss of information and necessitates the retyping of all of those often used paragraphs, names, and addresses. With a word processor, all of your information is remembered on disk, permanently. After you type in a document the first time, you simply save it onto a disk and that document is stored, but immediately available, forever. Whenever you need a print out of that document or a revision of it, you load it into your computer from the disk, modify it with your word processor, and print it out. Even those typewriters with bubble memories which don't forget when the power fails have limited usefulness in an office since they can hold only a small amount of text. A computer, with a disk drive, can hold many more documents inside itself than any electronic typewriter. The disk drive of a computer lets you easily save unlimited amounts of documentation onto as many disks as you need.

A word processor lets you make typographical mistakes without having any pressure for erasing and retyping. You can type along at fast speeds without worrying about errors. After you have typed in your entire text, then you can take your time when going back over the document to edit and fix errors through the use of the word processor's editing features. Only after you have made the document look exactly like you want do you print it out. Many word processors also have features such as word counters, spelling checkers, and a thesaurus.

In order for a computer to be a good business word processor, it should have a typewriter style keyboard. This will allow a typist to feel comfortable on the computer. A computer should also have a large amount of RAM so that you can run highly developed and user friendly word processing programs. These word processors have more features for easily manipulating words and will hold more pages of text. The capacity and speed of the disk drive are also important. The storage capacity of a disk drive will determine exactly how many pages you can save on a disk before you run out of space and have to insert a new disk. The faster a drive is, the less time you will waste waiting for programs and files to load and run. The quality of your hardcopies is totally determined by the quality of your printer.

The quality of a word processor is extremely important in a professional setting where ease of use and high productivity are needed. The C-128 is an excellent word processing machine for several important reasons. First, it has a standard typewriter style, full stroke keyboard so that a typist can make an easy transition to the computer. It has also been ergonomically designed; its keyboard slant will let you type faster for longer periods. From a technical standpoint, the C-128 makes an excellent quality word processor for business uses because of its large amount of memory, its fast, large capacity disk drive, and its CP/M compatibility. The C-128's large memory will accommodate quality, feature filled word processing software. The 410K capacity of the 1571 disk drive will hold approximately 200 double-spaced typed pages on each disk, which means that you won't have to switch disks as often as you would with a smaller capacity drive.

Furthermore, it is important to have a computer which will work with printers of all brands and types. The C-128's serial port will connect with any serial printer. It also has many interfaces available which will let you use any parallel Centronics printer. You can also use an RS-232 printer connected through an external interface. The C-128's versatility will let you choose whatever kind of printer that you want: letter quality, dot matrix, or thermal.

Finally, the CP/M compatibility of the C-128 opens up a huge amount of proven business programs which provide a wide selection of word processors. It doesn't make sense to buy a computer only to discover that you have to spend hundreds of dollars on just one software program. The C-128 itself costs less than many IBM and Apple software programs. The CP/M and 128 mode software for your computer is high quality, but without the high price. Not all of the CP/M software will be sold where you buy your C-128. You might need to look in computer stores or contact public domain sources for software.

Students today, whether in college, in high schools, or even in elementary schools have opportunities for being more productive than students had just ten years ago. Stand alone personal computers weren't

121

even sold until 1978, and they cost far too much for either students or parents to afford at that time. Most college students have an ongoing stream of research papers and other theme essays due throughout their semesters at school. A word processor will help a student avoid those all night typing sessions, retyping page after page of rough drafts and still winding up with white-out spots. Simply type in one rough draft of a paper and from then on use the editing features of the word processor to revise it as many times as you want before printing it out. The C-128 is an excellent student computer, especially when you're thinking of word processing. Its cost, versatility, and compatibility with other computers and their hardware make this a solid choice. In addition, with the use of a modem, a student can use the C-128 to access databases for researching and then save the information for later use.

6.2 Database Management

Database management and word processing are considered to be the top two productivity uses for computers. Let's take a look at database management. A database is simply a collection of information. Database management software lets you organize and manipulate this information. Names, addresses, product numbers, prices, telephone numbers, inventory stock numbers, company names, client names, and billing information: keeping these lists updated and accessible for easy searching can be simplified through the use of a computerized database manager. A database is really only a filing system which your computer creates and your disks hold. If you have large amounts of information to keep track of, you will find that your computer and a database management program will make the job much easier. Of course, you still have to type in all of the information just as you would on filing cards, but the computerized filing system lets you keep track of more items and you have more cards.

The value of a database manager goes beyond its capacity for holding information, ease of use and fast retrieval of items. You can specifically search for particular items from your records and tell the computer to print out only those items that you select. You could, for example, order the computer to print out a list of those clients whose payments are more than 30 days overdue. Or, you could ask for a printout of the names of those customers who reside in a particular location, or who have similar buying patterns. The key here is the common element within the data. A database manager will look through thousands of individual files and thousands of items in those files, pick up the common element that you have requested, and then give you that information on the screen, printed out, or saved into a new disk file.

For the business person, this particular application is as necessary as word processing. In fact, most database programs have an interacting word processor which will allow you to create documents which will hold specific items from your database files. This is helpful when you want to create form letters for mailings to customers, or if you want to distribute lengthy reports to several different people.

Database managers are needed by more than just businesses. There are many uses for databases in schools and in the home. Instructors and administrators need a computerized database manager. A typical college instructor has at least four classes of up to 30 students each. Elementary and secondary teachers have even more classes to keep track of. A database manager will let a teacher keep his/her gradebook up to date, and have room to add personal comments and additional categories of student information. The administrator of a school has the same needs as a business user. Not only are there students to keep tabs on, but there are also inventory lists, expense accounts, payroll records, transportation records, and parent addresses, to name a few.

Home users who want to computerize their records will appreciate a database management system. As an example, you could enter vital information about all of your possessions onto a database. This would let you keep track of the product, brand name, cost, serial number, warranty expiration date, address to contact for repair and maintenance, the store that you bought the product from, and other items of information which you often have to know months after you have made a purchase. This example of home management is simply an inventory file that you make through the use of a database manager. This type of file would also be extremely valuable for getting information together for an insurance claim after a fire or theft. Something as simple as an address book is really a database containing ordered, sequential sets of data records, each of which is made up of separate fields (name, address, etc.) with each entry's last name used as a sort key. A computerized database makes it easier to keep the information in one neat and accessible location which can be updated easily. This is much better than a box full of notes with names and addresses.

The student's need for a database manager is not as crucial as for the business person or even the home manager; however, there will be times when a student can use this kind of application to help with the collection of data. When compiling bibliographies and notes for research projects, a database manager will be a big help. Rather than keeping notes and bibliographic information on various pieces of paper or shreds of library cards, you can become more organized by entering those scattered notes into a database. When it comes time to compile the bibliography, just let the database sort the sources alphabetically and then you can make the corrections to punctuation and format before you actually print out the final product.

The uses of the C-128 for data management are as varied as those for word processing. The C- 128 is an excellent database manager for many of the same reasons that it excels as a word processor. In addition to the features previously mentioned, the keyboard of the C-128 has a numeric keypad which will aid in entering numbers.

6.3 Spreadsheets

A spreadsheet is a computerized record keeper in which you can label columns and rows, enter numbers into the cells, and automatically calculate and recalculate answers to mathematical formulas specified in the spreadsheet. The spreadsheet helps the business person to keep track of income, expenditures, and profit analysis. An individual can use a computerized spreadsheet for keeping track of the monthly budget. Your imagination is the only limit on your spreadsheet use.

Primarily the realm of business users, spreadsheets are becoming more popular within the home as a way of keeping track of the family checking accounts, saving accounts, mortgage payments, and other financially relevant information. Whatever you have been doing on paper with a pencil and calculator, you can do faster and easier with a spreadsheet. The spreadsheet is extremely valuable as a tool for financial analysis such as determining whether certain scenarios are worth proceeding with or not. A spreadsheet will let you change any numeric entries and at the press of a key, have your entire row or column of data recalculated. You can view, save, and print out the results of unlimited varieties of situations. Then, you can decide which particular set of figures and conditions are the most efficient for your business or home.

The benefit here is speed. It takes so long to recalculate long strings of figures that in many cases it is prohibitive to even attempt the task by hand. Also, if you do it by hand, there are so many opportunities for mistakes. Small businesses and home investors are better off if they look at all of the possibilities before making financial decisions, and the spreadsheet is the best way to do this.

There are hundreds of specialized spreadsheet applications which will perform particular tasks. Accounting and finance programs abound for tasks such as accounts receivable, accounts payable, general ledgers, inventory, payroll, and other financial utilities which aid in performing specific calculations that you need performed repetitively. The C-128 is excellent for doing spreadsheets and other calculating functions because of its large memory, its numeric keypad, and the wide variety of software available for this application.

6.4 Graphmaking

Beyond word processing, database management, spreadsheets, and accounting programs, the C-128's graphics abilities add even more value to this computer. The C-128 lends itself to quality graphmaking because of its high resolution graphics and its large number of colors. The bit mapped graphics modes of the C-128 will give you the opportunity to run better quality business software so that you can integrate pie charts, bar graphs, and other kinds of business graphics into your ongoing reports.

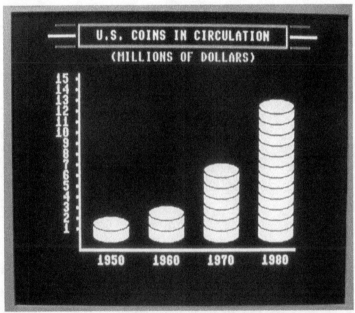

Fig. 6-2. Commodore C-128 Graph Making, 40-columns

The ability to create documents with visual displays of the information that you have gathered can be very important. Documents can be composed of a combination of text, numbers, and graphs. The most impressive reports combine all three. The best application software will provide a graphing option for use with your spreadsheet figures and your database information. By graphically representing data, it is often much easier for you to see exactly what trends are occurring in your business. Rather than analyzing a column of numbers, you can look at a chart or a graph which represents those numbers in relation to each other.

If you want to make printouts of pie charts be sure that you have a printer which will print out high resolution bit mapped graphics images. This type of a printer would be either a thermal or a dot matrix printer. Letter quality printers can print out bar graphs. Bar graphs are very useful and many businesses will not want or need to buy a separate printer which will produce colorful pie charts. All kinds of printers will work with the C-128, however, so you can implement whatever kind of printer arrangement that you wish.

6.5 Education

In 2019, online education is commonplace, and many well-established colleges and universities share their courses online. Because most of the online educational options from 1985 are no longer in existence, this section has been edited into past tense, although most of the text dates from the simpler days of 1985.

By 1985, Computer-assisted instruction was becoming more widely accepted by teachers, administrators, parents, and students. At first, the computer was used for teaching just computer skills and programming. By 1985, the computer could be used as a teacher's instructional aid in non-technical disciplines. For example, the computer is an excellent training tool for working on those academic skills which can be improved through practice or memory work such as grammar, math, and history lessons. The computer could free up the teacher's time and also added a new and interesting dimension for the student to interact with. Rather than having the teacher devote class time to remedial instruction with one or two students, these students could work on the computer using an appropriate program which would both instruct and drill them on the materials they need. There were also programs that teach exceptional students and ones that can be used by the entire class.

Microcomputers were continually becoming more involved in the educational process on every level, from stand alone training stations to multiuser networks. By 1985, an entire classroom of stand alone computers could be connected to the teacher's computer; the teacher can then monitor and interact with each individual computer station. Additionally, the computer was now being used by many people for home educational purposes. Software was priced low enough that parents could keep their children stocked with appropriate lessons to enhance their school work. This provided a good way for parents to become more involved with their children's education. Adults can take courses missed in their formal education through the use of their home computer, too. Many adults are going back to school on their computers.

The C-128 has enough memory built in to accommodate various programming languages, such as Cobol, Pascal, and C. Its CP/M capability allowed schools to acquire these programming languages immediately and at very low prices. The 128K memory, with the option of adding up to an additional 512K, could open up more educational applications. For example, the added RAM module could be used as a frame buffer for storing graphics data for animation and movies. It also could be filled with a dictionary or encyclopedia of 30,000 or more words. This would allow for instantaneous spelling checking during word processing activities. The C-128 has a keyboard which would appeal to the instructors who wanted to train their students in word processing. The numeric keypad would benefit the business and accounting instructors. Administrators as well could use the C-128 for the business side of their schools.

Commodore Supports Education

Commodore Business Machines, Inc. had a strong respect for the educational applications of their computers. They have several national and international projects underway which encourage excellence in education and they actively contribute hardware, software, and technical support to school systems throughout the U.S. and Canada. Commodore has also supported home use for educational purposes through its own software offerings and through its online educational project available through CompuServe.

In 1984, Commodore donated 1,000 computer systems and educational software to schools in 16 states. In 1985, Commodore's State Department of Education Donation Program will give over a million dollars worth of computer equipment and software to over 36 state Departments of Education across the United States. Commodore plans to donate C-128s to many school systems as part of this project. Over the past two years, Commodore has sponsored the international Olympics of the Mind competition. The Olympics of the Mind was an extra-curricular contest in which 150,000 students from over four thousand schools around the world participated in problem solving competition. In addition, Commodore had sponsored educational ceremonies which honor teachers and school systems across the nation.

Online Educational Assistance

Commodore implemented a telecommunications self-support network, called Educational Resource Centers (ERC), on CompuServe. ERC provided educational and technical support for educators. There were well over 500 schools and colleges (public and private) participating in this online project. The Commodore Education Special

Interest Group acted as an electronic bulletin board service for Commodore-using schools. Participants could share information about educational software, curriculum planning, and teaching strategies.

Other Online Educational Options

C-128 owners had a unique opportunity to take courses on their computers in the comfort of their own homes. TeleLearning, Inc. was an online educational network that provides coursework on personal computers. The C-128 was one of the computers that TeleLearning supports. Through TeleLearning's Electronic University, people could take courses on a wide variety of subjects and at various levels of learning. Children could benefit from online tutorials in the basics. Adults could take personal improvement and career advancement courses. People could even take college courses and study towards undergraduate and graduate degrees from colleges and universities.

See Chapter 7.6: Historical Guide to Online Services in 1985 for more discussion of the C-128 for education and the role that Commodore computers played in the early development of online distance education

Educational Software for the C-128

There are hundreds of educational software producers for the C-128. These companies provide software for all ages and on all topics of study. Much educational software produced for personal computers is home based and provided on a single disk or cartridge. This is usually very affordable and is readily available in computer stores, from mass merchandisers, and through mail order firms. There is also a great deal of educational software which is produced with the school market in mind. This kind of educational software is usually more expensive because it is intended to cover an entire curriculum for a course of instruction. For example, a secondary school mathematics course could contain up to 36 lessons bringing the student from decimals and whole numbers all the way through polynomial equations.

This ends the historical study of C-128 productivity from the 1985 perspective. I still use my C-128 for word processing. The 80-column display makes it very good for writing and it brings me back to a simpler time (although this 300-page book is not being written on a C-128 by me right now).   There are several 80-column word processors available online for the C-128 and they are free. I use Speedscript 128. There is also RunScript. Both of these were from Commodore magazines, Compute! and RUN. There are also commercially produced word processors that you can find online for free.   For example, Word Writer 128, from Timeworks, is an excellent 80-column word processor for the C-128. It was one of the first word processors that had drop down menus: a real advanced feature back then. Chapter 9 discusses where you can get software for your C-128 these days.

   Before we leave this chapter, let's take a quick look at entertainment software.

6.6 Entertainment On The C-128

No matter what serious applications that you will use your computer for, you will probably want to have your favorite entertainment programs handy. A benefit of a personal computer such as the C-128 is that it offers opportunities for entertainment for your whole family and even for a break at the office. The color graphics, split screen capabilities, sound, and large amount of memory serve to equip the C-128 as a great entertainment computer.

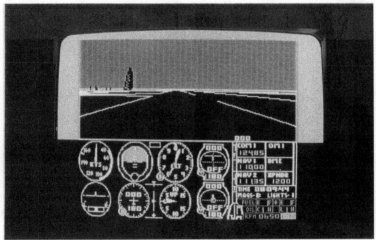

Fig. 6-3. C-128 64 mode Flight Simulator Software

Games aren't limited to arcade type shoot-em ups though there are certainly plenty of these fast action games available. You will find large memory interactive games being made for the C-128 that are not possible to run on smaller memory computers. You can even participate in game playing on your C-128 without having to buy software. An online network, such as PlayNet, will provide you with interactive colorful games that you can play online with others across the nation. You simply log onto PlayNet and ask someone to join you in a game. Then, you both move to a separate game playing room where you can chat with each other while you are playing the game. This is a way to meet people and it makes your game playing much more interesting than just playing against the computer. See Chapter 7 for more information on PlayNet.

133

In 1985, it was thought that, initially, the majority of entertainment software for the C-128, of course, would be for the C-64 mode. But, the outlook was optimistic for development of a good number of 128 mode games as time went along. As it turned out, the majority of games developers continued to develop only for the C-64, as is also the case today.

Fig. 7-1. Telecommunications on the C-128
(photo does not show phone line from the modem
"Line" port to the wall jack)

Chapter 7

Telecommunications on the C-128

In 1985, telecommunications at an affordable price was becoming available to home computer users and small businesses. Prior to that, it was considered to be an application for business research, investment analysis, and economic news. Larger businesses with the money to spend on expensive telecommunications equipment were accessing the online realm and had an edge over small businesses and individuals. The Internet was unheard of by the public at the time of the release of the C-128. In another 10 years, the Internet became available to home computer users.

Back then, your only option for going online was to have a modem (often only a 300 or 1200 baud modem) and a telephone line. Commodore users could dial into Bulletin Board Systems (BBSs) and they could dial into the larger online networks that were springing up. Back then, you could do many of the same activities as you do today: e-mail, chat (text-based), message boards/forums, downloading files, real time messaging, accessing news, among other things.

In the 21st century, modems are a thing of the past for many. Most people access the Internet through an Ethernet connection or a wireless network on their modern devices. The C-128 can also go online with an Ethernet connection or wireless. We will get into that later in this chapter. Today, there is a lot that you can do online with the C-128. It is different from what you are used to with your modern day computer and web browser. You do not get the photo quality images and online videos as you are used to today, but you can get Commodore graphics (PETSCII) when accessing a Commodore BBS and ASCII/ANSI graphics when accessing a non-Commodore system. This type of art work is popular and can be very detailed. Aside from that, you can do many of the same type of activities that online users do today.

This chapter includes information for modem users, as well as information on how to access present day online services through an Ethernet cable or wireless network, using your C-128.

7.1 Introduction to Telecommunications

If you want to experience dial-up or if you do not have Ethernet or WiFi ability in your area, you can use an old fashioned modem to go online. There are BBSs, UNIX shells, and larger networks that still allow access with a modem. Before getting into particulars about the modems that you might be using on your Commodore, a brief look at the terminology employed in this area will be helpful.

Telecommunications Jargon

When a computer is connected to another computer via telephone lines, it is said to be online. A modem (modulator-demodulator) is a device that allows two or more computers to communicate over the telephone lines by taking one computer's electronic impulses in the form of zeros and ones, translating them into modulating signals that a telephone can understand, and then retranslating them back into the electronic digital impulses that the other computer can understand. Computers don't have to be the same brand or size to communicate with each other.

A *terminal program* is the software needed to turn your computer into a terminal so that it can send and receive information through a modem. There are two kinds of terminal programs: dumb and smart. *Smart terminal* programs open up your computer's RAM memory for storage of incoming information and allow you to save information received onto a disk, tape, or to a printer. The storage area is called the *buffer*. If you hope to keep a permanent record of any telecommunicating, you will need a smart terminal. A *dumb terminal* will only let you view incoming information. You can't capture it in the computer's buffer for further processing. *Uploading* information is sending data from your computer to another computer's buffer.

Downloading is when your computer is capturing this information. These activities can only be accomplished if both computers involved have a smart terminal program.

A *packet-switched network* is a telephone network that handles communications between different kinds of computers. If you subscribe to a national information system, you are given the phone number of a packet-switched network in your local area (called a local node). This cuts down on your phone bills because you pay for a phone call to the local node rather than for a direct phone call to the mainframe of the online service you are calling. If you are close enough to your local node, your call might even be toll-free. Tymnet, Telenet, and DataPac were three such networks.

The *host computer* is the computer that you will access for your information. *Connect time* refers to the rate charged by national information systems when you are connected with their host computers. Many online information systems back in 1985, such as CompuServe, Delphi, and Dialog, were available nationwide through the use of packet-switched networks. The hourly rate varied depending on when you logged on: prime time (usually 8am to 6pm) or non-prime time (after work hours). Local bulletin board services usually provide free service and are operated by a system operator (sysop) who is an individual home computer user (not necessarily a C-128 user). Local online services range from offering computer user group information to community help services.

Terminal Settings

You should be aware of six settings on your terminal software before you go online. Most terminal programs are already preset for communication with the major online services, so you may never have to touch these settings; however, if you are having trouble sending and receiving information, you may have to alter some of these settings. In most cases, this is accomplished through menu selections from within the terminal program.

Your modem must be able to send and receive information. This capability is called *duplex* communication. Most of your communication will require *full duplex* mode, which is two way communication in which your screen displays what you are typing, as well as what is being typed on the other computer. (On the other hand, *half duplex* allows you to see just what is typed on the other computer.) You will usually be making the call, so you will set your program or modem to *originate*. *Baud rate* refers to the rate of data transmission in bits per second. The 1660 Modem/300 runs at 300 bits per second; the 1670 Modem/1200 runs at 1200 bits per second. *Word length* refers to the number of bits used to form one character (not the number of characters per word) and will usually be set to 8. *Stop bits* are signals that tell the answering computer that it has just received all the bits needed to form a single character. This is usually set to 1. *Parity* is used by computers for error checking. A typical configuration is 8 data bits, no parity, and 1 stop bit.

7.2 Commodore Modems

In 1985, Commodore produced their own line of modems. The 1660 Modem/300 and 1670 Modem/1200 were being sold at that time. You could also use third party modems, but usually they required a separate RS-232 interface, which you could buy from third party producers.

Commodore 1660 Modem/300

The 300 baud Modem/300 is Bell 103 compatible; it was based on the most widespread modem standard in 1985. Nearly all of the major national information services back then accommodated 300 baud modems, thereby making the C-128 accessible to almost everything available at that time. This modem connects directly to the user port of the C-128. It has a built-in speaker so that you can hear the phone as it dials and makes a connection. It also has an answer and originate switch on it so that you can set your modem for either activity.

Fig. 7-2. Commodore 1660 Modem/300

Commodore 1670 Modem/1200

The Commodore 1670 Modem/1200 provides a 1200 baud rate for much faster data communications. This modem uses the "AT" Hayes command protocol. There is a built-in speaker to let you hear the number as it is being dialed, and you can use both touch tone and rotary phones. The Modem/1200 offers auto answer, auto dial, auto baud setting, auto speed, and auto mode selection.

Both of the Commodore modems plug directly into the user port of the C-128 and your phone line is attached to the back of the modem.

Fig. 7-3. Commodore 167 Modem / 1200

As with the other Commodore modems that were bought new in the 1985 era, there was a free subscription to CompuServe and the Dow Jones News/Retrieval included.

7.3 Logging into a Retro BBS with a Modem

These days, if you have a Commodore modem, it is probably 30+ years old or thereabouts and you probably did not get a terminal program with your used modem. New Commodore modems did provide their own terminal program. If you do not have a terminal program, you will need to download one to get started. For 128 mode, there is Desterm 128 which supports dial up. For 64 mode, there are many. Often recommended are NovaTerm 9.6 and CCGMS 2017v.6 . These are available for download from various sites, such as commodoreserver.com, csdb.dk, commodore.software, and everythingcommodore.com You will also need a land line telephone; not a cell phone.

There are a lot of BBSs out there, which are mostly accessible via telnet (which we will discuss later in this chapter), but some are accessible through dial-up. For an updated list of Commodore BBSs, you should take a look at the "Commodore BBS Outpost" at cbbsoutpost.servebbs.com.   The "Telnet BBS Guide", located at www.telnetbbsguide.com, has another list of active BBSs. And, there is also the "BBS Nexus" at www.bbsnexus.com.   They provide a listing of BBSs that include both non-Commodore and Commodore systems, which are accessible through telnet and some through dial-up. Remember that a C-128 is capable of accessing most online systems, regardless of what computer they are running on; you don't have to dial into a system that is running on a Commodore computer.

We used a Commodore 1670 Modem/1200 to develop this section. This is the modem that most people with a C-128 would use. We haven't tried this with the many other modems that could also be used.

To get started with your modem, plug it into your user port with the computer off. Plug the phone line from the wall jack into the back of the modem, into the port marked "Line". Turn on your C-128. The modem should give a beep. Then, load and run your terminal program and fill in the configuration settings. Depending on what terminal program you are using, you will have many or few settings. You first want to set the Baud rate to match the speed of your modem.   Often, the default settings of your

Commodore-compatible terminal program will serve to get you going, but you may have to make some changes. Do a bit of research into the settings of the target (host) system; you will want to set your terminal to match the target system. For example, if you are calling a non-Commodore BBS, you might need to change the terminal type to ANSI or VT-100 (there are others), depending on what the host system uses. If you are calling a Commodore BBS, use PETSCII as your terminal type: this will allow you to view the Commodore graphics correctly. You should use the protocol settings mentioned earlier in this chapter for word length, stop bits, and parity. Follow the menu items in your terminal and when ready, select Dial Out or Auto Dial - it will have different names.

When your modem has dialed into the host and has connected, you will hear a continuous squealing sound from your modem's speaker. This tells you that your call is being answered. Wait a bit at this point for your modem and the receiving modem to communicate and establish a connection. After the connection has successfully been completed, the squealing will stop and you will receive questions from the remote system. Most systems will ask if you are a new user and will bring you through a series of start up questions to create your account and to inform the host system of the hardware you are using.

If you find that your modem won't connect, you might want to check your phone line. If the phone line is "noisy", that can prevent a connection. You can test your phone line by picking up the phone and dialing "1". If you have a noisy line, you will hear static. A good line should be quiet when you dial "1".

DesTerm 128

Here is a sample log-in session to a non-Commodore BBS, using a Commodore 1670 modem with DesTerm 128. Since I am using a 1200 baud modem, the first thing to do is to change the baud rate in the terminal to 1200. The 1670 modem is Hayes-compatible, so also set the terminal to Hayes. In the "Modem Settings" of DesTerm, select Hayes/1670 Setup and change Maximum Baud Rate to 1200. In the "Protocol Settings", change Baud Rate to 1200. Then enter "Terminal Mode".

With DesTerm 128 (I am using v2.01; there is a newer version) loaded and running, make the adjustments mentioned above. DesTerm 128 runs in 80-columns in 128 mode. The Help key gives you a help screen. CTRL/RUNSTOP gives you the Main Menu where you can make any adjustments that you need.

Hayes-compatible modems use AT commands. You can either have the terminal program automatically dial or you can manually type in the commands from terminal mode. In this sample session, we are calling the Back To The Future BBS (see web site bttfbbs.com or the Telnet BBS Guide for phone number).

In this example, I am entering the AT modem commands manually. From terminal mode, type:


```
atdt 1,##########
```

[the phone number of the BBS)

You should hear a short dial tone, then the number being dialed, a squeal, and some silence...


```
CONNECT 1200
Connected to bttfbbs

A graphics screen displays.

Login as 'new' to create an account.
Forgot password?  Login as 'reset'.

Login:

Password:
```


Then, another graphics screen will be drawn and a menu will display. The ANSI mode works for me. Follow the menu selections from there. If the graphics do not display well in some of the games, there is a menu item that let's you experiment with other modes. BTTF BBS offers a variety of things to do, such as reading/posting in message boards, reading news from the Sysop *(system operator), games, IRC (Internet Relay Chat), a dial-out modem option, weather forecast, among other things.*

Some commonly used AT commands that you might want to remember are:

+++ *Escape. Interrupts a telecommunications session by taking the modem out of terminal mode and putting it into command mode where you can issue more commands, or hang up.*

ath *Hang up modem.*

atz *Zap. Resets modem to default settings*

ato *Returns you to terminal mode*

atdt *Dial a phone number using touchtone method*

The AT commands and more information about the 1670 modem are provided in the "Commodore Modem 1200 User's Manual". This can be downloaded from Zimmers.net (see Commodore>Files section) or from the Internet Archive (archive.org). You can also get a more detailed listing of AT commands for Hayes-compatible modems by doing a simple search for Hayes AT commands.

This has been a short sample showing a typical log-in session using a modem with the C-128. Next, we will discuss an Ethernet cable connection.

7.4 Going online Today through an Ethernet cable connection

The majority of C-128 users will not use a modem to access the online world. In this section, we will discuss using the C-128 with an Ethernet cable connection. There are several companies that produce devices that allow you to go online through an Ethernet cable connection or with a WiFi modem.

I have the 64NIC+ Ethernet interface from RETRO Innovations. This device plugs into the expansion/cartridge port; the Ethernet cable plugs into the 64NIC+. The 64NIC+ offers 10-megabit Ethernet connectivity, RR-NET compatibility, NET64/TFE compatibility, and C-64 and C-128 compatibility. Aside from the Ethernet ability, the 64NIC+ includes a Reset switch for resetting the computer, plus a lot of technical features that go beyond this discussion. But, I will mention them in case you are interested. It has an onboard optional ROM socket for autoboot functionality; the ROM socket can accommodate up 256KB ROMs; it has an optional rotary switch which can select 1 of 16 ROM images; the cartridge can be configured to reside in either IO1 or IO2 address spaces; and it can be configured to reside in any 16 byte address bank within the IO address space. For this discussion, we are focusing only on its Ethernet capability.

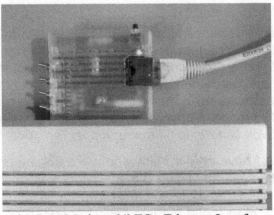

Fig. 7-4. Modern 64NIC+ Ethernet Interface

The 64NIC+ (pictured above) is simple to use. You plug the device into the expansion port and attach your Ethernet cable to it. You will need to get software, such as a terminal program, that is compatible with RR-NET/NET64/TFE.

I use the 64NIC+ primarily for "telnet". Telnet is defined by telnet.org as "both a network protocol and an application that uses that protocol. Most often, telnet is used to connect to remote computers and issue commands on those computers. It's like a remote control for the Internet." You can telnet into BBSs, MUDs (Multi-User Dimension or Domain -- this is a multiplayer, real-time virtual world in which you would do role-playing in a fantasy type setting), check the weather, play games, access library card catalogs, log into a UNIX Shell, do e-mail, chat, among other things. For a detailed list of places to telnet to, see Telnet.org (www.telnet.org). This includes many more places other than BBSs. The 64NIC+ will let you do a lot more than just telnet: your software will define what you can and cannot do. See next section for more discussion on this.

For more information about RETRO Innovations and the 64NIC+, visit go4retro.com. You can order this and other products that work with the C-128 from their web site store at store.go4retro.com/. Located in the United States. RETRO Innovations welcomes suggestions for new product ideas.

KipperTerm

You need a telnet client program to be able to telnet into the Internet. KipperTerm includes a telnet client program. (A 'client' means that you are the one telnetting into some other place, as opposed to a telnet 'server' which would be the host that receives incoming telnet callers). There is an 80-column version that you can run in 128 mode: KipperTerm 128. And, there is a 40-column version that you can run in 64 mode: KipperTerm 64.

Although I have only a black and white display on my C-128 system in 80-columns, I find the 80-columns is good for online activities, such as doing e-mail, browsing the Web using Lynx (a text-based browser), and reading message boards and news. Of course, you might have color in your 80-column display, especially easy if you have one of the Commodore monitors, and so you would get color with KipperTerm 128. If you want to experience a colorful BBS and you don't have an RGBI color monitor, you can always use KipperTerm 64, which has a 40-column color display.

With the 64NIC+ attached and the Ethernet cable connected, turn on the C-128 and boot up the terminal program. For KipperTerm 128, it will display "KIPPERTERM 128 and Initializing RR-NET" and then open a window that is the Main Menu. The Main Menu includes various Function key definitions for the terminal, and below that, it automatically displays technical information about your Ethernet connection. I won't include my own data below, but yours will automatically show up.

```
Interface: RR-NET
MAC Address
IP Address
Netmask
Gateway
DNS Server
TFTP Server
DHCP Server
```

All of this information is automatically detected and displayed for you.

The Function keys in KipperTerm 128 include:

```
F1: Telnet
F3: Gopher
F5: Address Book
F7: Config
F8: Credits
```

A popular option for accessing online tools and surfing the Web is through a UNIX Shell account. C-128 users can do this. On a UNIX shell system, you can do e-mail and you can access the Web, using the a text-based web browser, Lynx. There are other online activities other than through the World Wide Web, such as Telnet, Internet Relay Chat (IRC), File Transfer (FTP),

149

Gopher (similar to, but different than a web site), text-adventure games, reading news, and more, that you can access with your C-128. (You can also access BBSs through an Ethernet connection on your C-128.)

In both cases, you can use telnet to get where you want to go. In order to telnet to someplace, you simply press F1. That will bring you to the following display which brings you through a couple of questions. Let's say that I want to access my UNIX Shell system, SDF.ORG. Here's what I would do after pressing F1:

```
telnet
hostname (leave blank to quit)
: sdf.org

resolving sdf.org
port # (leave blank for default)
:    [I leave it blank and just hit Return]
mode - V=vt100,  A=ascii (ANSI),  P=petscii
```

[here you press either V, A, or P. Since SDF.ORG is not a Commodore system, you can use either V or A. I just hit A for ascii, but V for vt100 also works. If you were accessing a Commodore system, such as a BBS, you would hit P for petscii here. Petscii will allow you to view the Commodore graphics.]

After you select your terminal display type, you get this:

```
connecting in ascii/ANSI mode
KipperTerm 128(c) 2015 Sean Peck

ok

sdf.lonestar.org (pts/89)
if new, login 'new' ..

login: [here you type your user name or 'new',
if you are a first time user]
Password for [you@sdf]:  xxxxxxx
```

Once you are inside the shell, you will see this:

```
$
```

Most people will see this $ and say, "what do I do now?!" If you are new to a UNIX Shell account, you will be wondering what to do next. At the $ prompt, type 'help' and that will get you going. You will find that you can do lots of things. It is worth doing some preliminary study on how to utilize a UNIX Shell before you log in. For SDF.ORG, you can read up on what they offer and study some how-to's by going to www.sdf.org and printing some help files with your other computer. Just a thought.

Gopher

You might have noticed that there was a Function key for "gopher" in the KipperTerm main menu. As defined on SDF.ORG, "Gopher is a network protocol that enables multiple servers to create a single, uniform file system that transcends system architecure and operating systems (GOPHERSPACE). With GOPHER, information holds the most value. Since presentation is uniform across GOPHERSPACE, the user does not encounter any challenges in 'learning' a new site. Because of its simplicity and its emphasis on the importance of informational texts, GOPHER is ideal for those who are visually impaired." Through

151

SDF.ORG, you can create your own gopher site. For information about developing a gopher site on SDF.ORG, type "gopher" at the $ prompt. (You can also create your own Web site.)

KipperTerm 128 (and KipperTerm 64) has a gopher client, which means that you can access a gopher site from KipperTerm, similar to how you use telnet. You can get a list of gopher sites at www.ucc.asn.au/~alastair/gopher.html .

There is more to KipperTerm, but this gets you going.

Aside from the terminal program, KipperTerm, there is also Contiki (2016): an operating system that you can use for Internet applications. It includes telnet, web browser, web server, IRC (Internet Relay Chat), and WGET (to download files from the Internet). You can get more information about Contiki online at www.c64-wiki.com and at contiki-os.org. These are compatible with the 64NIC+.

Let's move ahead and take a look at going online with a wireless modem on the C-128.

7.5 Going online through a WiFi connection

A third method of going online with your C-128 is with a wireless modem. There are several producers of wireless modems. I am using the WiModem from CBMStuff. Referred to as an Internet modem, the WiModem connects to the user port of the C-128, thus freeing up the cartridge port. It can be used with a wide range of Commodore computers. It allows you to connect to the Internet with a standard Commodore 128 or 64 terminal program, giving you more options for choice of terminal.

The WiModem (pictured below) emulates a standard Hayes-compatible modem. It comes configured with 300 baud as the default baud rate and can be increased up to 9600 baud. (It can run up to 38400 baud when using Commodore Server software, V1541. See commodoreserver.com for a discussion of that server.) For most connections, I use 1200, which is plenty fast for what I do. I have tested it in 128 mode with an 80-column display (using DesTerm 128) and also in 64 mode with a 40-column display. For this section, I am using the 64 mode and NovaTerm 9.6.

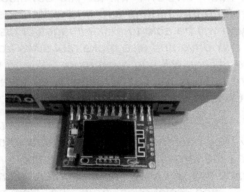

Fig. 7-5. Modern WiFi WiModem

To get started, turn on your wireless router. With power off, insert the WiModem into the user port. Then, turn on the C-128. Load and run the terminal program, in my case, NovaTerm 9.6 in 64 mode. When you use the WiModem for the first time, you will need to do some preliminaries in order to connect to your router. After you have done the initial setup to your router, the modem remembers the data and thereafter, you don't need to keep reentering the basic data. CBMStuff provides a detailed manual, which explains what to do to get connected to your router. This entails entering several AT commands into your terminal. We won't duplicate all of the installation commands here. Refer to the manual, which is available on the CBMStuff.com web site.

A very important point to remember is that the baud rate of your terminal program must match the baud rate of the WiModem, in order for any AT commands to be typed. So, remember that the modem is at 300 baud by default, which means that you need to change your terminal program to 300 baud first. That allows you to type commands into the terminal, both to initially set up the router connection and later to go online. If you forget to do this, you will waste a lot of time trying to type something and nothing displays and nothing happens. Later, you can raise the baud rate of the WiModem and your terminal, if you wish. Just make sure they match.

At the time of this writing, the WiModem developer, Jim Drew, is working on two new programs for this device: WIHD and WICOPY. Jim explains: "WIHD is like a fast loader for the disk drive, except it's for accessing the 3MB of on-board storage that the WiModem has. WICOPY will let you download and upload disk images from/to the Internet to/from the WiModem's on-board storage, and you will be able to make images of disks using your 1541 or 1571 disk drive and also make real disks from image files (.d64)." These utilities will add even more value to the WiModem and offer more options for C-128 users when dealing with disk images. See Chapter 9 for a discussion of disk images.

CBMStuff does more than develop products for the Commodore. They host the Commodore Retro eXpo (aka CRX). CRX, known as the largest gathering of Commodore enthusiasts in the U.S., provides a venue for presenters of new products, special guests, and celebrities from the Commodore world. Display areas show modern hardware being used with original Commodore systems. For more information about this annual three-day event, see www.crxevent.com.

For more information about CBMStuff and the WiModem, visit cbmstuff.com. CBMStuff sells the WiModem through their web site. Located in the United States.

NovaTerm 9.6

You can download the terminal program from various locations online, such as commodoreserver.com or ftp.zimmers.net. Remembering that the default is 300, the first thing to do is to match up the baud rates between the WiModem and NovaTerm. So, for example, if NovaTerm boots up in 1200 baud, you need to change that to 300 baud right away. Do this from terminal mode by pressing the Commodore key+R (C= denotes "Commodore key from here on; don't type the "+"). The baud rate is displayed at the top of the screen and C=+R toggles the rates. Toggle to 300. Then, you will be able to type into the terminal. This is where you type in the AT commands for your initial setup to your router from the manual. Make sure that the terminal program is in ASCII mode when you first do the router installation (press C=A to toggle between ASCII and Graphics - the top title bar of your terminal screen; second from the left to right - "T" will be highlighted if it is in ASCII mode; not highlighted if in Graphics mode). This setting is important during initial router setup because the SSID and password of the router are case sensitive and if you are in Graphics mode, upper and lower cases are reversed. There are three different methods of connecting to your router, so if one doesn't work, you can try another.

After you have made the connection with your router, then you can increase your baud rate. For example, to increase the baud rate to 1200, type at*b1200. That changes the baud on your modem. Then, press C=+R until the top of the screen displays 1200. Now, we have matched up the modem and the terminal at a speedier baud rate.

With your WiModem connected to your router, first test out your wireless connection, by typing:

```
atdt google.com:80
```

If your modem and router are connected properly, you should get this:

```
connect 1200
```

To hang up the connection and be allowed to enter more AT commands, type:

```
+++
```

To hang up the modem, type:

```
ath
```

Then the following will be displayed:

```
no carrier
```

Now you are ready to travel somewhere with your C-128 and WiModem. For our sample session, let's visit the ParticlesBBS, a Commodore BBS, which runs on a C-128 computer. Before accessing the BBS, we want to set our terminal to be compatible with their system. There are a few initial settings that you make from terminal mode. You do this by pressing the Commodore key, abbreviated C=, on the lower left side of the keyboard, and the letter key designated below:

C= T   (Term = should be set to "Commodore")

C= A   (Toggle "Graphics" mode)

C= C   (Toggles 40 or 80 columns; we want 40)

Those are the basics.

To make the modem go to Particles BBS, type:

```
atdt particlesbbs. dyndns. org:6400
```

You can get this and other BBS addresses from the Commodore BBS Outpost listing mentioned earlier. The first part of the address is the domain, followed with a colon and the port number of 6400. The port number is important since that is configured on the BBS end and your command needs to match that. If you don't include the port number, the default modem setting of 1541 will activate, and that won't get you where you want to go in this case.

After you type the ATDT address, you will get the following:

```
connect 1200

A short message from the BBS and hit Return:

Do you support Commodore Color/GFX? (type "y")

Do you want 40 or 80 columns? (type "4" for 40c)
```

Then you will see the ParticlesBBS start up screen followed with prompts to enter your Handle, Number or New. As a new member, type new and follow the prompts to create an account. From then on, there is a menu system that you follow to move throughout the BBS.

There are a variety of things you can go on the system: e-mail, message forums, grafitti wall of one-liners, text files, online games, chat with sysop (Mr. Ice Breaker), feedback to sysop, search for a user, voting booth, news about the BBS, information, terminal settings, configure account, file transfers, and list of recent callers. The BBS serves a variety of retro computer systems. It is a friendly BBS and typical of many BBSs that you might experience with your C-128. When you log off, you will notice "+++" displayed at the very end and "no carrier".   (By typing "ath", you will make absolutely sure to hang up the connection and should be ready for your next trip.)

This ends our look at the WiModem and accessing a Commodore BBS through a wireless Internet connection.

7.6 Historical Guide to Online Services in 1985

In 1985, there were many general interest services which provided a bit of everything, and there were many other online services which provided highly specialized information on almost any topic. There was no Internet for the public at that time. Four major general interest services available then were CompuServe, the Dow Jones News/Retrieval, The Source, and Delphi. For Commodore-specific users, QuantumLink came out in 1985 and became a haven for C-64 and C-128 users. For historical purposes, this section will give you a brief rundown of some of the online services that were available in 1985.

Fig. 7-6. Historical Guide to Online Services

General Interest Online Services

CompuServe

CompuServe Information Service (CompuServe) was the largest and one of the most popular online information services in the U.S. and Canada. It provided a variety of databases and opportunities for consumer activities and communication. Popular services for communication purposes included the CB Simulator, the Forums (special interest groups), the National Bulletin Board, and EasyPlex, an electronic mail service. Transactional services, such as electronic shopping and banking, were offered. Facilities for detailed research on a wide variety of topics were available from many databases. The Executive Information Service (EIS) of CompuServe was also quite popular, but was targeted at individual business people and professionals, providing business communications, worldwide news and updates, demographic and sales information, travel assistance, and banking and brokerage services.

Dow Jones News/Retrieval

The Dow Jones News/Retrieval (DJN/R) was the most respected information service in the areas of business and finance information. Traditionally, large businesses and stock investors have accessed DJN/R for current national and international news, stock quotes, and corporation profiles. In 1985, DJN/R had broadened its offerings to appeal to people who have interests in areas beyond the business and economic fields. You could choose from a wide selection of general consumer, research, and news services, as well as MCI Mail. Thirty-six database services were available of which a third were general interest and non-business.

The Source

The Source was another very large general purpose information service offering plenty of opportunity for communication, consumer activities, and traditional research. There were five major headings within The Source: Communications, News and Information, Investor Services, Travel and Leisure, and Personal Computing Services. Almost 75% of its membership was composed of business people and professionals.

Delphi

Delphi was one of the most popular of the general interest online information services. Similar in certain respects to CompuServe, The Source, and the Dow Jones News/Retrieval, Delphi was an information, communications, and entertainment system. You could get information on news, weather, sports, stocks, commodities, money markets, banking, shopping, and travel arrangements, as well as electronic mail. Delphi offered access to Dialog, a research library offering 200 databases. You could also send electronic mail from Delphi to subscribers of other online services such as The Source and CompuServe. Delphi had an active Commodore Special Interest Group, the Flagship Commodore, which offered specific programs and information for the C-128.

QuantumLink

QuantumLink was set up specifically for Commodore computer users by Commodore Business Machines and Quantum Computer Services. QuantumLink was like a blend of CompuServe and PlayNet. Commodore Information Network programs and many other general interest services were available on QuantumLink. QuantumLink was software specific and was tailored to take advantage of the C-64/128's sound and color graphics. The software included a terminal for automatic logging onto the network and came with the purchase of the Commodore 1660 and 1670 modems.

For Q-Link users who would like to relive the Q-Link experience, Q-Link Reloaded is available in 2019. Information is currently available online at 1200baud.wordpress.com/q-link-reloaded/.

Viewtron

Viewtron was a colorful and informative service which also provided custom software for the C-128. Viewtron offered many services devoted to Commodore owners, including software and hardware reviews as well as online shopping. An online auction was an on-going part of Viewtron. This feature allowed users nationwide to bid on a wide variety of consumer products as well as C-128 specific items.

Entertainment Online Services

PlayNet

PlayNet provided communication and entertainment services for its wide range of users. While entertainment and social interaction services were available on most online general interest services, PlayNet was different in that it was tailored totally to the social dimensions of personal computing. Subscribers could use PlayNet as an easy way to meet new people and talk to them about any topic without the barriers of distance and physical appearance. The person-to-person socialization accomplished on PlayNet was highlighted by its large bank of interactive games. PlayNet members could chat in a public reception area or in private, and they could select playing partners for games such as backgammon, boxes, checkers, chess, bridge, and many more. These games were in full color and took advantage of the Commodore's graphics and sound capabilities. PlayNet's services also included electronic mail, a shopping center, bulletin boards, and the ability to upload and download programs and files.

People/Link

People/Link was also tailored specifically to the goal of providing entertainment and socialization for its members. Calling itself an "electronic playground", People/Link offered many avenues for people to interact either privately or as a group. Its offerings included Netmail, an electronic mail service; Partyline, which featured live interactive communication with other members; Peoplescan, a national bulletin board, allowed users to post notices on any topic, and buy, sell, or trade anything they want; and Club-Link, which let you start your own club. Also offered were games, such as bridge, blackjack, chess, backgammon, and checkers - all with high resolution color graphics; Catch-a-Star, an electronic gossip column which featured live online interviews with famous people; The On-Line Herald, People/Link's monthly news magazine; and Who-is-who, a directory of subscribers.

Education Online

Education has always been affected by advances in technology. In 1985, schools were already using the microcomputer in the classroom to provide primary and supplemental instruction in many non-technical disciplines such as social sciences, business, and composition. While educators in traditional school settings were designing effective plans for computer-assisted instruction back in 1985, another group of educators was implementing its teaching strategies over the telecommunications lines.

One company participating in this online teaching for Commodore computerists was TeleLearning Systems, Inc.. Students could take courses to be used for credit towards degrees from other colleges and universities across the nation. Services included not only regular course work, but also seminars, counseling, and access to an electronic library.

In early 1986, I designed and operated educational services in the Learning Center on Q-Link. I ran the Tutoring Center where we offered nightly tutoring sessions in realtime. This was the first realtime online tutoring service that was nationally available. It was soon followed with the Q-Link Community College where we offered non-credit courses. Both of these services were precursors to the boom in online education that has occurred in the 21st century. More information about these educational services and future developments in online education can be found online at CALCampus, an online school that grew from the seeds planted on Q-Link. See www.calcampus.edu/research.htm for a detailed history, documenting the early days of online education and the role of Commodore computers.

Online Mail Services

Nearly every information service that you could access in 1985 had some sort of mail service. Many provided electronic mail for use by subscribers, allowing them to send and receive messages to each other. Two intra-utility services were EasyPlex from CompuServe and SourceMail from The Source. There were, however, more versatile mail services which let you send mail to people without a computer and to any location in the world. Two of these were MCI Mail and EasyLink.

MCI Mail

Through MCI Mail, you could use your C-128 to create and send letters, memos, reports, invoices, and proposals to anyone in the continental U.S., and you could access Telex for worldwide communications. After you had created and sent your document online, it was electronically transmitted to an MCI Mail postal center closest to the addressee. There, it was laser printed, packaged and delivered. Other MCI Mail subscribers would receive your electronic messages instantly. You could also choose four-hour or overnight delivery to non-subscribers. You could send MCI Mail overseas. Your letter was transmitted electronically and printed overseas. From there, it could be delivered to over 80 countries by courier or by the local postal system. MCI Mail was available to all Dow Jones News/Retrieval customers.

EasyLink

EasyLink was similar to MCI Mail. C-128 owners could access this online service which provided instant mail service to EasyLink subscribers within the U.S. or to any Telex user worldwide. You could also send written correspondence to people who did not have a computer or were outside of the EasyLink network. You could choose from telegrams delivered in hours, Mailgram messages delivered the next business day, domestic computer letters delivered by first class mail, and international cablegrams with overnight delivery.

This ends our historical look at the online services that were available for Commodore users back in the 80s. These days, of course, you can do all of the above and more online through the Internet on the World Wide Web.

Fig. 8-1. C-128 For Programmers

Chapter 8

For Programmers

Commodore packaged a very good programming manual with the C-128 which would help you get on your way, and for more serious programming, the Commodore 128 Programmer's Reference Guide is available. This chapter will not teach you how to program. In this chapter, we will discuss the capabilities of the built-in BASIC 7.0 of the 128 mode, provide a rundown of the commands, as well as the other programming possibilities. The C-128 has one of the most advanced versions of Microsoft BASIC ever to be built into an 8-bit computer, including a built-in machine language monitor program and a sprite editor. Schools will be interested in what the C-128 offers programmers, which includes teaching not only BASIC, but also other programming languages such as Pascal, C, Cobol, and Assembly language.

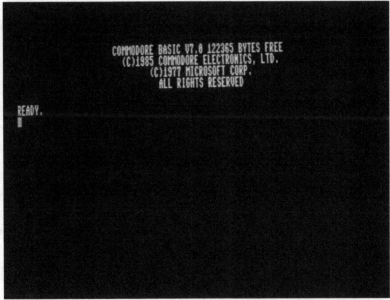

Fig. 8-2. C-128 Startup Screen (80 columns) BASIC 7.0

8.1 Introduction to BASIC 7.0

BASIC is the acronym for Beginners All-Purpose Symbolic Instruction Code. This is the computer language most used among home computerists, primarily because it was the industry standard and was provided with most home and personal computers.

The C-128 holds the features of the C-64 which placed that computer at the top of the worldwide home computer market. The features most appreciated by people and which were different from other home computers were the color graphics modes, sprite capabilities, animation capabilities and polyphonic sound.

Although the C-64 was much better than its competitors and became the most popular home computer in the world, it did have some drawbacks for programmers. The difficulty in implementing color, graphics, sprites, animation, and sound was one criticism directed against the C-64. People wanted to be able to manipulate its features with easy-to-use commands and statements from BASIC. Commodore's engineers and designers addressed these particular shortcomings of the C-64 when designing the C-128.

The 128 mode has all of the capabilities of the C-64, but without the difficulty of implementing them. In addition, it has up to 512K available to take advantage of the color graphics and sound in ways not possible on a computer with smaller memory. Commodore took a most extraordinary step in designing the BASIC for this computer. It listened to its user base, and it combined all of the best features of its other successful computers, not just the C-64. People familiar with Commodore computers will recognize many of the disk and file handling commands in BASIC 7.0. The disk command syntax used in the C-64 was retained in ROM only to ensure compatibility with existing C-64 software. The 128 mode, however, holds many more disk access commands which are far more versatile and user-friendly. Many of these were retained from the still popular BASIC 4.0 of the CBM 8032 and SuperPET.

The C-128 benefits from more than the experience gained from the C-64, the CBM 8032, and the SuperPET. Many of the programming aids and the built-in machine language monitor of the Plus/4 and C-16 have been included. Programmers will find the C-128 a pleasure for program development because of features like the automatic line numbering, automatic renumbering of programs, easy calls to machine language subroutines from within BASIC programs, and many more. BASIC 7.0 also holds brand new commands which were not possible to use on previous computers. For example, three new commands for handling the added RAM memory will be appreciated by programmers.

As you read through this chapter, you will gain an awareness of the programming versatility of this computer. Let's begin with its graphics modes.

8.2 Graphics Capabilities

The keyboard of the C-128 demonstrates the graphics versatility of this computer. The keyboard itself can be used to create graphics displays in sixteen different colors. Many of the keys have two graphic designs on their front surfaces. To activate the right side graphic, you press the Shift key in conjunction with the particular key. To activate the left side graphic, you press the Commodore key with your chosen key. When used within Print statements inside a BASIC program, these keyboard graphics designs can create impressive displays. The C-128 also gives you access to two separate keyboard modes: upper case with graphics characters and lower/upper case with graphics. The keyboard is easily toggled between these two modes by pressing the Commodore and Shift keys together. These keyboard features make the C-128 unique. Furthermore, the 128 mode offers six different display modes plus eight multicolored sprites, all with sixteen colors to choose from.

Text Displays

In text mode, you can display characters such as letters, numbers, special symbols and the keyboard graphics characters. The C-128 gives you two text displays to work with: 40-column with high resolution graphics and 80-column text with keyboard graphics.

The text mode offers access to all sixteen colors at once. If you have a television or a composite monitor, you can take advantage of the 40 column by 25 row screen display. All of the keyboard graphics characters are available within this mode, but you can't mix lower and upper case text with graphics characters.

If you have an RGB monitor or a monochrome monitor, you can obtain an 80-column text display from the C-128. When you are in 80-column mode, high resolution bit mapped graphics with 640 by 200 resolution is available and functional, but you must use pokes and peeks for controlling it. Most people will be using the 80-column capability for business applications and correspondence which will utilize letters and numbers. While using an 80-column display, you can mix all of the keyboard characters, both lower and upper case as well as graphics characters, while utilizing all 16 colors if you want.

Both 40 and 80 column text modes have a window statement which lets programmers define custom sized windows and place them anywhere on the screen. Multiple windows can be placed per screen, each with its own activity taking place inside. When combined with the split screen graphics capabilities, this allows for combining high resolution graphics and sprites and windows on the same screen.

Graphics Displays

When using the 40-column display, you have access to two high resolution bit mapped graphics modes. There is Standard Bit Mapped Mode available which offers a resolution of 320 by 200 pixels with sixteen colors to choose from. When in this mode, you have control over the placement and coloring of each individual pixel on the screen. Each pixel can have one of two colors: one foreground and one background.

The second high resolution graphics mode is called Multicolor Bit Mapped Mode. This mode offers a resolution of 160 by 200. Each pixel can he one of four colors within an 8 by 8 pixel grid. These four colors are composed of three foreground colors and one background color, selected from any of the sixteen colors available.

Split Screen Displays

The 128 mode offers programmers a blend of text and graphics in 40-column mode. A Split Screen display is offered in Standard or MultiColor Bit Mapped modes when using a television or a composite monitor. This gives you the ability to have text displayed on the same screen as the bit mapped color graphics and sprites.

Sprites

Sprites are custom created objects which can be placed anywhere on screen within any mode of graphics operation. These creations can be colored and animated through the use of several easy to use commands within BASIC 7.0. Up to eight sprites can be defined and animated on one screen. Sprites can move in front of or behind other sprites and screen objects. BASIC 7.0 has three ways of detecting collisions among sprites and other screen objects.

What are sprites used for? Many software companies use sprites for game development. Sprites make excellent moveable components for games. They can also be used for more serious applications such as in educational software and in some business applications. Sprite programming in BASIC 7.0 will be discussed later in this chapter.

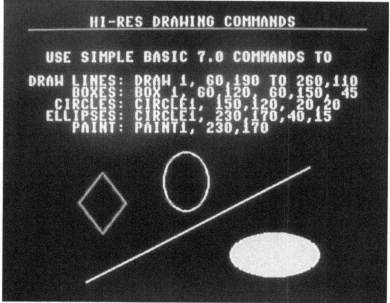

Fig. 8-3. C-128 Hi-Res Graphics (40 columns)

8.3 Graphics Commands and Statements

The C-128 has many graphics commands built into its BASIC which make manipulating graphics and text displays quite easy. Let's go through some of them.

In the following section, commands and statements are in upper case. Arguments (also known as parameters) are in lower case letters. Square brackets [ ] hold optional arguments. Angle brackets < > show required arguments where the programmer must choose one. Ellipsis (...) shows that an argument may be repeated.

COLOR source #, color

COLOR is used to tell the computer which of seven color sources you want to activate and which of the colors you want displayed. The source number can range from 0 to 6. The number following the source refers to one of 16 possible colors. Setting the color parameters is the first step in graphics programming.

What follows are the seven Color Source numbers:

0   40 Column Background
1   40 Column Foreground Graphics Screen (Standard Bit Map)
2   Foreground Graphics #1 (Multicolor)
3   Foreground Graphics #2 (Multicolor)
4   40 Column Border
5   Character Color (40 or 80 Column)
6   80 Column Background Color

Example: COLOR 0, 5

This would activate the 40 column background area and would color it purple.(Note: Color codes are listed in the Appendices.)

GRAPHIC mode[,C][,S]

GRAPHIC is used to select one of the six screen display modes. The mode can be a number from 0 to 5.

0   40 Column Text
1   Standard Bit Map
2   Standard Bit Map: Split Screen
3   Multicolor Bit Map
4   Multicolor Bit Map: Split Screen
5   80 Column Text

C can be either 0 or 1. 1 clears the graphics screen; 0 doesn't. S refers to the particular line number that you want to start displaying text on when in split screen mode.

Example: GRAPHIC 2, 1, 20

This would activate a Standard Bit Mapped Split Screen. The 2 turns on the graphics mode; the 1 clears the bit mapped screen in preparation for the upcoming display; the 20 tells the computer to print any text on the twentieth line.

In order to use any of the high resolution drawing and painting commands, you must issue the Graphic command first.

GRAPHIC CLR

GRAPHIC CLR will clear the memory allocated for high resolution graphics, thus freeing up 8 to 9 K of reserved RAM memory.

LOCATE X,Y

LOCATE is used to position the pixel cursor anywhere on the bit mapped screen. X is the horizontal coordinate in a 0-319 range. Y is the vertical coordinate in a 0-199 range. You can't see the pixel cursor on screen unless you use the RDOT function. LOCATE is sometimes used to begin a series of DRAW commands, otherwise it's an optional command and not necessary for using the other graphics drawing commands.

CIRCLE [color source],A1,B1[,XR][,YR][,SA][,EA][,ANG][,INC]

CIRCLE has up to nine parameters that can be used. This command is very versatile and can be used for drawing all kinds of geometric designs. The color source can range from 0-3. A1 and B1 are the column

174

and row coordinates for the center of the circle. XR is the horizontal coordinate for the radius; YR is the vertical coordinate for the radius. SA is the starting arc; EA is the ending arc. ANG is the clockwise rotation. INC is the increment of degrees between segments.

Example: CIRCLE 1, 250, 50, 35

This will draw an ellipse with radii 50,35 starting at the screen location of 250,50.

All nine parameters are not required for using the Circle command; however, in order to tap its versatility for creating other geometric designs, you will want to use them all.

BOX [color source],A1,B1[,A2,B2][,Angle][,Paint]

BOX is used for drawing geometric shapes which have four straight sides. This can be used not only for squares and rectangles, but also for drawing parallelogram and rhombus shapes. The color source can be 0-3 (0=background, 1=foreground, 2=multicolor 1, 3=multicolor 2). Al and Bl are the upper left corner coordinates; A2 and B2, the lower right corner coordinates. An angle can be given which will rotate the shape clockwise. A paint parameter is optional: 0 is off and 1 is on.

Example: BOX 1, 100, 100, 150, 150

This would create a square with each side 50 pixels long. On the standard bit mapped screen, a square starting at point 100,100 and extending down to 150,150 will appear in whatever color has been previously set by COLOR.

DRAW [color source],A1,B1[TO A2,B2]...

DRAW is very flexible and can be used for drawing all kinds of geometric shapes. This essentially connects as many points with one continuous line as you specify. You specify a starting point with A1,B1 and then specify the line's direction through the subsequent column and row coordinates. You may place as many sets of points to be connected as you wish.

Example: DRAW 1, 10, 10 TO 80, 80

This will draw a line on a standard bit mapped screen with the specified coordinates.

WIDTH X

WIDTH is used for setting the width of lines used in drawing functions. X can be 1 for normal or 2 for double width lines.

PAINT [color source],A,B[,Mode]

PAINT will fill in any area which has been encompassed by lines of the foreground color specified. A and B are coordinates of a point lying inside the shape you want filled. Mode refers to the area defined by color source selected or any non-background source. Be sure not to fill the area with the same color as the background because you won't see your shape.

Examples: PAINT 1, 120, 135

This will fill in the box that you created above.

PAINT 1, 250, 45

This will fill the ellipse that you created earlier with the CIRCLE command.

CHAR [color source],X,Y[,String][,Reverse Flag]

CHAR acts like a Print statement on a text display. You can print textual material on a high resolution bit mapped screen by using this statement.

Example: CHAR 1, 11, 10, "GRAPHICS SAMPLES", 1

This will display the quoted words on a bit mapped screen in a reversed field, in column 11 and row 10. If no Reverse Flag is set, it defaults to your prior color settings.

Sample Program

Here is a sample graphics program from the <u>Commodore 128</u> <u>System Guide</u> (page 106), which illustrates the commands: COLOR, GRAPHIC, CIRCLE, BOX, DRAW, PAINT, CHAR. You can download the <u>System Guide</u> from various sites online, such as

archive.org/details/C128SystemGuide

or

commodore.ca/manuals/128_system_guide/toc.htm.

In 128 mode with a 40-column display, type each line, followed with a Return to enter the line. After you have typed the entire program, type LIST to see your completed program. Type RUN to run the program.

If there is a typo, you will get an error message along with the line number. Fix it. Use the CRSR keys to move to where the problem is. Remember from Section 5.1 to press SHIFT to make it go up or to the left. If you need to insert a character, press SHIFT and INST DEL at the same time to insert blank spaces. Then you are able to type in what you want. Press RETURN to log in the fixed line. Once the program works, save your program for future reference. (Refer to Appendix E, the DSAVE command). REM statements are comments and are not run as part of the program. Punctuation is critical. Type the commas, colons, and semicolons exactly as printed in the lines below.

```
5 REM C-128 SYSTEM GUIDE PAGE 106
10 COLOR 0,1:REM SELECT BKGRND COLOR
20 COLOR 1,3:REM SELECT FORGRND COLOR
30 COLOR 4,1:REM SELECT BORDER COLOR
40 GRAPHIC 1,1: REM SELECT STND HI RES
60 CIRCLE ,150,130,40,40:REM CIRCLE
70 COLOR 1,6:REM CHANGE FORGRND COLOR
80 BOX ,20,100,80,160,90,1:REM BOX
90 COLOR 1,9:REM CHANGE FORGRND COLOR
100 BOX ,220,100,280,160,90,0: REM BOX
110 COLOR 1,8:REM CHANGE FORGRND COLOR
120 DRAW 1,20,180 TO 280,180:REM DRAW LINE
130 DRAW 1,10,20 TO 300,20 TO 150,80 TO 10,20:REM DRAW
            TRIANGLE
```

```
140 COLOR 1,15:REM CHANGE FORGRND COLOR
150 DRAW 1,150,175:REM DRAW 1 POINT
160 PAINT 1,150,97:REM PAINT CIRCLE
170 COLOR 1,5:REM CHANGE FORGRND COLOR
180 PAINT 1,50,25:REM PAINT TRIANGLE
190 COLOR 1,7:REM CHANGE FORGRND COLOR
200 PAINT 1,225,125:REM PAINT BOX
210 COLOR 1,11:REM CHANGE FORGRND COLOR
220 CHAR,11,24,"GRAPHICS EXAMPLE":REM DISPLAY TEXT
230 FOR I=1 TO 5000:NEXT:GRAPHIC 0,1;COLOR 1,2
```

Line 230 delays the program for a while and then switches back to text mode, colors the characters black, and ends the program. If you want the graphics to remain on the screen, omit the GRAPHIC statement in this line.

Two more BASIC 7.0 commands are of interest to programmers:

SCALE 1 o r 0 [,XMAX,YMAX]

SCALE will let you enlarge or decrease the size of your graphics creations on the bit mapped screen. 1=on. 0-off.

WINDOW TLC,TLR,BRC,BRR[,Clear]

Programmers will enjoy the ease by which they can set multiple screen windows from within their programs. Although a window can't hold high resolution graphics, it can be used on the same screen with high res graphics through the use of the split screen modes, and it can hold graphics and animation created by the keyboard graphics sets.

TLC and BRC are the top left and bottom right column coordinates, between 0-39 for a 40 column display and 0-79 for an 80-column display. TLR and BRR are the row coordinates and can be anywhere from 0-24. You can clear a window by setting the last parameter to 1.

Many windows can be placed on one screen. Once you define a window, all subsequent output is directed to that window until another window is created. You can make your program move among windows with the use of several branching commands available in BASIC 7.0.

8.4 Sprites

Sprites are moveable graphics objects which you can design into any shape and can be displayed anywhere on a 40 column screen without affecting any other displayed features. They can be single or multicolored from a choice of 16 colors. The C-128 can accommodate up to eight sprites on screen at once, and there is complete collision detection among sprites.

Fig. 8-4. C-128 Sprites

There are three ways to design sprites in 128 mode. Masochists can use the 64 mode using a tangle of poke commands. We will discuss the two methods that most people will use in the 128 mode. You can design your sprites using the standard graphics statements previously discussed, or design them through the use of the C-128's built-in sprite editor.

The first method of creating and animating sprites lets you use the new drawing commands provided by BASIC 7.0. You draw your sprites through the use of the standard graphics commands and keep each sprite's size within the prescribed limits. Your sprite can take up a 24 by 21 pixel square for standard sprites and a 12 by 21 pixel square for multicolored sprites. Once you have drawn a sprite on the screen within the limited area, you have four statements available for achieving your finalized sprite:

179

SSHAPE, SPRSAV, SPRITE, and MOVSPR.

You use the SSHAPE command to store the picture data into a string variable. The data is then transferred from a string variable into a sprite so that it can be manipulated. This is accomplished through the use of the SPRSAV statement. When you have created and transferred the sprite data into a sprite, you can then turn it on, color it, select standard or multicolor mode, and expand it through the use of the SPRITE statement.

SSHAPE A$,Al,B1[,A2,B2]

The coordinates Al and B1 are for the upper right corner of the sprite grid. A2 and B2 are the opposite corner's coordinates. A$ is the name of the string variable into which you have stored your sprite data. The coordinates of this statement have to exactly match those of the original sprite drawing. Essentially, this statement stores the bit mapped image of the sprite in the string variable A$ for later processing.

SPRSAV A$,Sprite

This statement transfers the picture data from A$ into the specified sprite data area so that you can turn it on, color it, and animate later.

SPRITE <#>[,O][,C][,P][,X][,Y][,M]

This is the statement which actually makes the sprite do something. The parameters from left to right are:
  # Sprite Number from 1 to 8
  O On or Off
     If 0 = 1 then sprite is turned on.
     If 0 = 0 then sprite remains off.
  C Color (1 to 16)
  P Priority
     If P = 0 then the sprite is in front of screen objects.
     If P = 1 then the sprite is behind other objects.
  X Expanding horizontally:
     If X = 1 then the sprite is expanded horizontally.
     If X = 0 then the sprite is a normal size.
  Y Expanding vertically:

If Y = 1 then the sprite is expanded vertically.

If Y = 0 then it remains the normal size.

M   Select Standard or Multicolor sprite.

If M = 1 then multicolored.

If M = 0 then standard mode.

The last statement in this particular sprite procedure is MOVSPR which is used for moving the sprites that you have created.

MOVSPR Sprite #,X,Y

This statement places the numbered sprite at an absolute position on the screen on coordinates X and Y.

MOVSPR Sprite #,Angle # (0-15)

This statement is actually used to move the sprite numbered. The Angle can range from 0 to 360. The # refers to the speed of movement, from 0 to 15.

The procedure outlined above can be programmed into a BASIC program. When the program is run, all of the steps are activated in sequence, resulting in the animation of the newly designed sprite.

The second method for creating and animating sprites is through the use of the C-128's built-in sprite editor which is accessed with the command SPRDEF. When you issue this command, the C-128 will display a sprite grid on screen and prompt you for the sprite number (1 to 8). Once you have entered the particular number of the sprite that you want to design, the grid will be activated and your sprite number displayed in the upper left corner. The sprite work area is a grid of 24 by 21 screen characters, each character block referring to a pixel once the sprite has been translated into a bit mapped image. The sprite editor holds commands which can be used to create, color, expand, and save sprite information.

The commands available within the sprite editor follow:

KEYS	FUNCTIONS
CLR	Erases the work area.
M	Turns off or on a multicolor sprite.
CTRL(1-8)	Select sprite foreground color (1-8).
C= (1-8)	Select sprite foreground color (9-16).
1	Turns on pixels in the background color.
2	Turns on pixels in the foreground color.
3	Turns on areas in multicolor1.
4	Turns on areas in multicolor2.
A	Turns on or off automatic cursor movement.
CRSR	Moves the cursor (+) within the work area grid.
RETURN	Moves cursor to the start of the next line.
HOME	Moves cursor to the top left corner of the grid.
X	Expands sprite horizontally.
Y	Expands sprite vertically.
Shift RETURN	Saves sprite from grid and returns computer to sprite # prompt.
C	Copies one sprite to another.
STOP	Turns off displayed sprite and returns to sprite # prompt without changing the sprite.
RETURN	(at sprite number prompt) Exits SPRDEF mode.

Remember, C= means the Commodore key

When you have finished creating your sprite, save it with the Shift-Return command. The sprite data is automatically saved within a reserved area in memory. If you want to create several sprites, just reenter the sprite editor by typing in another sprite number. Follow the same procedure as with the first sprite. Once you have finished all of the sprite designs that you want to do, you leave the sprite definition mode by pressing the Return key at the Sprite Number prompt.

The creative part done with, now you must program the computer to display the sprite data. The SPRITE and MOVSPR commands are used for activating the individual sprites. These commands are placed within the context of a BASIC program, and saved the same as any other program. In order to reuse your sprite data, you must save that also. This is done using the BSAVE command which saves the sprite data in a binary file on disk. A programming line within your BASIC program using the BLOAD command will automatically load the sprite data into the C-128's memory whenever you want to run your program using the sprites that you have created.

The BASIC 7.0 of the C-128 will also allow you to create adjoining sprites. This is useful when you want to create a sprite which is larger than the 24 by 21 pixel grid. In order to accomplish this, you will use method one, utilizing the standard graphics statements in conjunction with the sprite statements SSHAPE, SPRSAV, SPRITE, and MOVSPR.

SPRCOLOR is used to set multicolored sprites. It can assign any of the 16 colors to each of the two possible multicolored sprite colors.

Another BASIC 7.0 statement used with sprite programming is COLLISION. COLLISION defines three types of interrupts: sprite-to-sprite collision, sprite-to-display data collision, and light pen. This statement will branch program execution to another line when certain collision circumstances have occurred. The BUMP function is used to tell which sprites have collided since the last check.

The sprites, high resolution graphics, split screen modes, drawing commands, and keyboard graphics designs will be appreciated by software developers and home programmers. You can make the computer perform highly intricate screen designs and animation by combining text with high resolution graphics and sprites, and placing them on screen along with text windows.

Now, let's take a look at the sound and music commands of BASIC 7.0.

8.5 Sound Commands and Statements

The C-128 has a built-in advanced sound synthesizer, the Sound Interface Device (SID), which is the same 6581 chip used in the C-64. (Later, Commodore came out with the 8580 SID, which slightly differs in sound.) This chip allows programmers and musicians to create their own sound effects, musical pieces and also to code sheet music onto the computer. The difference between sound on the C-128 and on the C-64 is in the way you can control the SID chip; BASIC 7.0 offers many commands for programming it. Additionally, the SID chip can be programmed with Machine Language.

Back in the 1980s, the SID chip quickly became famous as a tool for digital sound production, and it has remained highly regarded by professional music makers who continue to develop intricate music and sound effects. This section of the Handbook includes a discussion of the BASIC 7.0 commands for sound production. For more detailed instruction on programming the SID chip, you should refer to the two manuals published by Commodore: Commodore 128 Programmer's Reference Guide and also the Commodore 128 System Guide. Both are available for download from various web sites. In addition to the programming manuals from Commodore, there have been other books published dealing with the SID chip. Take a look at archive.org.

The C-128 can produce musical tones which cover a full nine octaves using three separate voices simultaneously. Sounds can be output through television speakers or through external speakers. Each of the three voices has many settings which you can control. These include control of the quality of the sounds produced, known as the waveforms. There are four possible waveforms which can be set for each voice: triangle, sawtooth, variable pulse, and noise. The SID chip also lets you control volume parameters dealing with attack, decay, sustain, and release of a sound (ADSR). A filter option also exists so that you may control other subtleties of sounds.

You may duplicate any instrument that you wish; however, the C-128 already has done the hard work of figuring out specific parameters for ten different instruments: piano, accordion, calliope, drum, flute, guitar, harpsichord, organ, trumpet, and xylophone. If you want to play a piano, for example, you simply activate a single envelope setting (0), rather than having to calculate the values of the parameters to duplicate the sound of a piano.

The C-128 provides six BASIC programming statements for controlling music and sound effects: SOUND, ENVELOPE, VOL, TEMPO, PLAY, and FILTER. These six actually do much more than just control six elements of a sound. When used simultaneously with three voices and when all of the particular options are utilized for each statement, you actually have control of closer to one hundred individual aspects that contribute to a single musical score.

Let's take a look at the six sound statements built into BASIC 7.0.

SOUND VC, FREQ, DUR[,DIR][,MIN][,SV][,WF][,PW]

The Sound statement is valuable because of its versatility and is used most frequently for producing sound effects rather than songs. The parameters are defined below:

VC	Select VOICE (1,2, or 3)
FREQ	Set the FREQUENCY (pitch) of a sound (0-65535)
DUR	Set the DURATION for playing a sound (in sixtieths of a second)
DIR	Set the SWEEP DIRECTION in which a sound is incremented or decremented (0-2)
MIN	Set MINIMUM SWEEP FREQUENCY (0-65535), if the Sweep Direction has been set
SV	Choose the STEP VALUE for SWEEP, the increment specified in the Direction parameter (0-32767)
WF	Select WAVEFORM (quality of sound)

0	Triangle
1	Sawtooth
2	Variable Pulse
3	White Noise

PW	PULSE WIDTH: width of the variable pulse waveform. If the Variable Pulse Waveform has been selected, the Pulse Width is also set.

Here is a sample program that illustrates the SOUND command of BASIC 7.0. Type it into 128 mode, press Return after each line, and SAVE it to your storage device for future reference. RUN the program.

185

If there is an error, the Line number will be displayed with the error message. Type LIST (the line number without parentheses). Type the correction into the line and press Return. Then SAVE the program again and RUN it.

This program generates random sounds. It illustrates how many thousands of sounds the SID chip can produce by using various combinations of the SOUND parameters. This sample program is from the Commodore 128 Programmer's Reference Guide (page 345) and the Commodore 128 System Guide (page 138). An in-depth discussion of the meaning of each line in this program is included in the System Guide on pages 138-139.

```
5 REM C-128 PROGRAMMERS REFERENCE GUIDE PAGE 345
10 DO
20 PRINT "VC    FREQ    DIR  MIN  SV    WF    PW    ":PRINT
30 V=INT(RND(1)*3)+1: REM VOICE
40 F=INT(RND(1)*65535):REM FREQUENCY
50 D=INT(RND(1)*32767):REM DURATION
60 DIR=INT(RND(1)*3):REM STEP DIRECTION/SWEEP
70 M=INT(RND(1)*65535):REM MIN SWEEP FREQ SINCE DIR IS
SPECIFIED
80 S=INT(RND(1)*32767):REM STEP VALUE
90 W=INT(RND(1)*4):REM WAVEFORM
100 P=INT(RND(1)*4095):REM PULSE WIDTH
110 PRINT V;  F; DIR; M; S; W; P:PRINT:PRINT
120 SOUND V, F, D, DIR, M, S, W, P
130 SLEEP 4
140 SOUND V, 0, 0, DIR, 0, 0, W, P
150 LOOP
```

Let's continue to look at more sound commands.

VOL X

VOL is one of the easiest to use. You may set the volume anywhere from 0 to 15, lowest to loudest.

ENVELOPE E[,A][,D][,S][,R][,WF][,PW]

ENVELOPE lets you set different controls in the SID chip. You can control the volume and quality of sounds with this statement, essentially

186

deciding which kind of instrument you will be playing and how it will sound.

The parameters for Envelope follow:

E	Envelope Number (0-9)
A	Attack (0-15)
D	Decay (0-15)
S	Sustain (0-15)
R	Release (0-15)
WF	Waveform (0-4)
PW	Pulse Width (0-4096)

Ten instruments have already been programmed into the C-128 and can be played simply by specifying their individual Envelope numbers (0-9) within a BASIC program. The ten instruments that you have available are outlined below.

Envelope Number	Instrument
0	PIANO
1	ACCORDIAN
2	CALLIOPE
3	DRUM
4	FLUTE
5	GUITAR
6	HARPSICHORD
7	ORGAN
8	TRUMPET
9	XYLOPHONE

These Envelope Numbers represent the preset values for ADSR, Waveform, and Pulse Width of the ten instruments listed.

The Attack, Decay, Sustain, and Release (ADSR) parameters actually control the quality of the volume at which you hear a sound. Attack refers to the speed at which a note rises to its fullest volume. Decay refers to the speed at which a note falls from its peak volume to its normal playing volume. Sustain is the normal volume at which a sound is supposed to be played. Release refers to the speed at which a note falls from its sustain volume to zero volume (end of the sound). With the Envelope statement, you can change each ADSR parameter up to 16 times.

187

TEMPO X

TEMPO lets you assign a speed to the playing of your songs. X can vary from 0 to 255, slowest to fastest. A default value of 8 is always in effect for the tempo.

PLAY "VN ON TN UN XN Elements"

PLAY is as powerful to the playing of notes as the Print statement is to the displaying of letters on the screen. They both follow the same syntax. The letters within the quotes of the Play statement represent the actual notes to be played.

For example, if you want to play Do-Re-Mi, then type PLAY "C D E" and press Return. The computer will play the three notes in succession. This is an elementary example, but should illustrate the ease by which BASIC 7.0 lets you play a song.

The parameters available within the Play statement follow:

VN	Voice Number (1,2 or 3)
ON	Octave Number (0 to 6)
TN	Tune Envelope Number (0 to 9)
	(The ten predefined instruments mentioned
	above are selected in this parameter.)
UN	Volume (0 to 15)
XN	Filter (On=1, Off=0)

Elements: The elements that control the duration of a note and its subtle sharpness or flatness can be set as follows:

#	Sharp
$	Flat
W	Whole Note
H	Half Note
Q	Quarter Note
I	Eighth Note
S	Sixteenth Note
.	Dotted Note
R	Rest between notes
M	Wait for a measure to finish before beginning the next.

All of the elements should come before the particular note being described, except for the Rest and Wait elements.

Fl LTER [FREQ][,LP][,BP][,HP][,RES]

FILTER adds even more versatility to the control you have when creating musical scores. Preceding the Play statement within a BASIC program, the Filter statement can modify the crispness and quality of the sounds that you have selected. Filter affects the harmonics of the waveforms being used.

Sounds can be filtered in three ways: low pass, band pass, and high pass. All three filter out frequencies above or below levels that you specify, thus producing varying effects on the sounds to be played. Tinny, hollow, full, or solid sounds can be produced through the use of a filter.

The cutoff frequency, the type of filter being used, and the resonance are controlled with FILTER.

FREQ	Cutoff frequency (0-2047)
LP	Low pass filter (0=Off, 1=On)
BP	Band pass filter (same)
HP	High pass filter (same)
RES	Resonance (0-15)

Three filters can be activated for each of the SID chip's three voices.

When used to their fullest, the six sound statements of BASIC 7.0 can produce intricate polyphonic songs as well as a wide range of sound effects. Not all of the statements and their parameters need be used when creating sounds.

Here is another sample program from the Commodore 128 System Guide (page 153). This illustrates the commands that have just been discussed. When you RUN the program, turn up your volume so that you can hear when the filter is on versus when it's off.

189

```
5 REM C-128 SYSTEM GUIDE PAGE 153
10 ENVELOPE 0, 5, 9, 2, 2, 2, 1700
15 VOL 8
20 TEMPO 10
25 PRINT "LINE30"
30 PLAY "C D E F G A B M"
35 FILTER 1200, 0, 0, 1, 10
40 PRINT "LINE 45 - FILTER OFF"
45 PLAY "V2 O5 T7 U5 XO C D E F G A B M"
50 PRINT "SAME AS LINE 45 - FILTER ON"
55 PLAY "V2 O5 T7 U5 X1 C D E F G A B M"
60 PRINT "LINE 65 - FILTER OFF"
65 PLAY "V3 O6 U7 T6 XO C D E F G A B M"
70 PRINT "SAME AS LINE 65 - FILTER ON"
75 PLAY "V3 O6 U7 T6 X1 C D E F G A B M"
80 PRINT "LINE 85 - FILTER OFF"
85 PLAY "V2 O6 TO U7 XO H CD Q EF I GA S B M"
90 PRINT "SAME AS LINE 85 - FILTER ON"
95 PLAY "V2 O6 TO U7 X1 H CD Q EF I GA S B M"
100 PRINT "LINE 105 - FILTER OFF"
105 PLAY "V1 O4 T4 U8 XO H .C D Q # EF I $ GA S .B M"
110 PRINT "SAME AS LINE 105 - FILTER ON"
115 PLAY "V1 O4 T4 U8 X1 H .C D Q # EF I $ GA S .B M"
```

This ends our discussion of the sound of music on the C-128.

8.6 Disk and File Handling Commands

People familiar with the CBM 8032 and SuperPet computers will recognize many of the disk and file handling commands in BASIC 7.0. The BASIC 4.0 of the CBM 8032 and SuperPet computers allows for easy manipulation of data files. It lends itself to one word disk access commands, such as Append, Backup, Catalog, Collect, and others. C-128's BASIC 7.0 has about thirty commands that can be used for program as well as file handling activities. It will also accept the commands used in C-64 BASIC. The C-128 file handling commands support program, sequential, relative, and user files. These commands can be used with single disk drives, double disk drives, or even a cassette drive. The BASIC 7.0 disk commands also work with the SD2IEC. For the command syntax, see Appendix E.

Disk Commands

BACKUP

The Backup command can be used to copy all files from one disk onto another. This is used only when you have two disk drives. The disk being copied to is automatically formatted with the Backup command.

CATALOG

CATALOG is issued to get a list of files held on a particular disk. The disk directory is displayed on screen and doesn't disturb any program which is in memory.

COLLECT

COLLECT is used to houseclean a disk, freeing up improperly used space on the disk. Any disk space that has been allocated to incorrectly closed files is made available for use, and all references to these files are deleted from the directory.

191

COPY

The Copy command is used for copying a single file from one disk onto another disk. It can also be used to make a duplicate file on the same disk under a new name.

DIRECTORY

This is essentially the same as CATALOG. It displays the directory of the current disk in the active drive.

DLOAD or F2

DLOAD will load a program from disk into the computer's memory, making it ready to run. This command is preprogrammed into Function Key 2 when you enter 128 mode. You may use DLOAD from within a BASIC program. When used with a string variable which has been defined within the program, DLOAD A$ will automatically load the program named in A$ from disk.

DSAVE or F4

DSAVE will save a program in memory onto the disk in the active drive. This command is preset onto Function Key 4 when you are in 128 mode.

LOAD and SAVE

Both of these commands can be used for disk loads and saves, although they are usually implemented for cassette loading and saving of programs.

HEADER

The Header command is used when you are using a disk for the first time. It creates the disk directory on a disk, assigns the disk a name and an identification number, and sets up the Block Availability Map. This command can be used for reformatting used disks. In this case, the files on the old disk are all erased, but the name and identification can be retained.

RENAME

The Rename command is used for giving an existing program a new name on the same disk.

RUN

By typing RUN followed by the name of a program in quotes, the computer will automatically load the specified program from disk and run it.

SCRATCH

SCRATCH is used for deleting a program or file from a disk.

File Handling Commands

There are many file handling commands which can be used in conjunction with disk commands. The C-128 can support program, sequential, relative, and user files. The following commands are helpful for writing programs which manipulate files.

APPEND

APPEND will open a disk file, reset its end of file pointers, and allow another file to be appended.

BOOT

This is used for automatically loading and running a binary file from disk.

BLOAD and BSAVE

These two commands were discussed in the sprite programming section. They are used for loading and saving binary files into any memory location.

CMD

CMD is used to divert output from the screen to an external device such as a printer or a disk drive, although it is most commonly used for printer output.

CONCAT

CONCAT is used for concatenating or merging two data files.

DCLEAR

DCLEAR clears all open channels to a specified disk drive unit.

DOPEN and DCLOSE

Both of these commands are used when accessing the disk drive for reading or writing files.

DVERIFY and VERIFY

This command makes the computer check the program on the specified drive against the program in memory, to verify that they match.

GET #, INPUT #, RECORD

All three of these statements are used for gathering information from a data file. GET # reads one character at a time from a previously opened disk or tape file. INPUT # reads information from a disk or tape file, but it reads entire strings at once rather than one character at a time. Both GET # and INPUT # can be used for reading sequential and relative files. RECORD allows you to position a relative file pointer to select any character of any record. This is used with relative files so that you can begin reading at any particular location.

OPEN and CLOSE

These are similar to DOPEN and DCLOSE, but can be used to access a cassette as well as a disk file.

PRINT

This is used to write data to a data file and can be output to disk, cassette, or printer. It can be used for sequential or relative files.

These commands will make your file handling very smooth. This ends our look at the disk and file handling commands.

8.7 Programming Aids

The C-128 benefited from the programming aids that were built into the Plus/4 and C-16 computers which were released in late 1984. These two home computers did not receive the attention that they warranted, primarily because critics focused on the mediocre built-in software applications of the Plus/4 rather than the highly advanced BASIC 3.5 that was also built into it. The C-128 holds all of the programming aids that were built into the BASIC 3.5 of the Plus/4. These include commands that allowed automatic line numbering, error detection, program renumbering, a built-in machine language monitor, automatic line deletion, and several useful looping functions.

Here is an overview of these programming aids.

AUTO

This command activates an automatic line numbering feature in the C-128 mode. You may specify the increment between line numbers.

DELETE

DELETE is used to erase a line or a group of lines from a BASIC program.

HELP

If you run into errors when you are writing a BASIC program, you can use the Help command. When HELP is used in 40-column mode, the line containing the error is listed and the particular error is highlighted. In 80-column mode, the error is underlined.

KEY

KEY is used to redefine the eight function keys of the 128 mode. All eight function keys are preprogrammed, but the Key command gives you more flexibility for defining keys to suit your particular purposes.

MONITOR

The C-128 holds an extensive machine language monitor which can be accessed with the Monitor command from direct mode.

RENUMBER

RENUMBER will let you renumber an entire BASIC program. It holds default values which will begin renumbering at line 10 in increments of 10. You can specify any starting line number and any increment.

TRAP and RESUME

TRAP and RESUME are used for locating errors within a BASIC program.

TRON and TROFF

TRON enables trace mode, while TROFF disables it. Both are used in program debugging.

Several advanced looping features are built into BASIC 7.0 which programmers will find useful. These help the programmer practice structured programming and are reminiscent of languages such as Pascal. The following looping features are in addition to the standard GOTO, GOSUB, and FOR/NEXT statements which most BASIC languages offer.

```
DO/LOOP     UNTIL..WHILE..EXIT
IF-THEN-ELSE
IF-THEN BEGIN. . .BEND:ELSE
```

8.8 Machine Language Monitor

The C-128 has a built-in machine language monitor program. This monitor program contains a machine language monitor, a mini assembler, and a disassembler. Many programmers will use the monitor to create subroutines to incorporate into larger BASIC programs. These subroutines are programmed in machine language in order to speed up the execution time of the program. Others will use the monitor to create entire programs. A machine language monitor program allows the user to modify the contents of memory in a computer. Not only can you enter and retrieve values from each memory location, but also you can load and save programs to and from specific memory locations. The machine language monitor of the C-128 holds the following commands:

A	ASSEMBLE	Enter assembly code.
C	COMPARE	Compares two sections of memory.
D	DISASSEMBLE	Disassembles 8502 machine code into assembly language.
F	FILL	Fills memory range with a specified byte.
G	GO	Begins execution of a program at specified starting address.
H	HUNT	Searches throughout a specified part of memory for all occurences of a byte.
J	JUMP	Jumps to subroutine.
L	LOAD	Loads a file from tape or disk into memory.
M	MEMORY	Displays a range of memory in hexadecimal and ASCII.
R	REGISTERS	Displays 8502 registers.
S	SAVE	Saves memory contents to tape or disk.
T	TRANSFER	Transfers code from one part of memory to another.
V	VERIFY	Compares memory values with those on tape or disk.
X	EXIT	Leaves MONITOR and returns to BASIC.
.		Assembles 8502 code.
>		Modifies 8 byte sections of memory.
;		Modifies 8502 register displays.
@		Displays disk status.

8.9 8502 Microprocessor Speed Commands

The C-128's advanced operation has led to the development of two new commands that directly control the speed of the computer's 8502 microprocessor. FAST will double the C-128's operating speed from 1 MHz to 2 MHz. All operations but I/O are sped up in this mode. Graphics can be manipulated in FAST mode, but you must slow down the 8502 before displaying them. SLOW will return the microprocessor to the 1MHZ speed of operation.

8.10 RAM Expansion Commands

The C-128's ability to have its 128K of RAM nearly tripled through an expansion cartridge has opened up the need for more commands. FETCH, STASH, and SWAP are present to allow programmers to easily take advantage of the additional memory.

FETCH directs the computer to go to a specified 64K bank in the RAM cartridge and retrieve data stored there. STASH commands the computer to move data from a specified 64K bank of internal RAM out into the expansion module. SWAP combines both operations and makes the computer swap information in and out of the RAM expansion module. The length of a block of data can be as large as 64K and can be accessed from any of the 64K banks of memory available both internally and in the expansion cartridge.

Furthermore, the C-128 has enough memory to accommodate other programming languages which are made available on disk or cartridge. These include Pascal, Logo, C, Cobol, Pilot, Forth, Comal, and others. The 128 mode isn't the only operating mode in which you can run other languages. The CP/M mode also accommodates many programming languages already developed and tested on other CP/M Plus computers. The 64 mode, too, can run other programming languages.

Not including the screen editing features, there are over 150 separate features built into BASIC 7.0 in the form of commands, statements, special programming aids, and functions. See Appendix E for the entire list.

This ends our chapter for programmers.

Fig. 9-1. Software

Chapter 9

Software, Disk Images, and More Information

In this chapter, you will learn where to acquire software, how to handle disk images, and where to look for more information about your C-128. Sections 9.1 through 9.3 relate entirely to current day information. Section 9.4 holds a combination of current day and historical details on where to find more information about the C-128.

If you are considering a purchase of a newly developed software program (or a peripheral) for the C-128, you will want to read up on what others who have bought the product are saying. Consider recommendations from friends, or members of a user's group, or read reviews posted in the various Commodore forums online, or watch a video review on YouTube. You can also ask people what they recommend on a forum or a BBS.

On the other hand, if you are considering which free program to download next, you might consider reading up on its description from the download site. Most download sites for Commodore programs include a brief write up about the program. If it's a free download and the program looks interesting to you, you might as well download it and give it a try. Current day C-128 users can acquire a large amount of software that was written back in the early years, for free. Games for the 64 mode, in particular, have a large following. You can find lists of top 10 to top 100 games and download many of them for free.

9.1 Where to get software for the Commodore 128

When acquiring software for the C-128, you will need to decide which operating system you want to use. C-64 programs will be the easiest to find since there are so many of them. Back in 1985, there were roughly 6,000 different software programs that ran in 64 mode. In 2019, there are many more, and new programs are still being developed. For the 128 mode, there are significantly fewer software programs available, because fewer were developed in the early years. But, still, you can find a good deal of software online. For example, you can buy original Commodore software from OldSoftware.com and on eBay. Also, if you buy an SD2IEC, you might be able to purchase or download software compilations for both the 128 and 64 modes, depending on the company. For CP/M mode, in 1985, there were approximately 10,000 commercial and public domain programs in existence. In 2019, it is probably a similar number since CP/M was overtaken by MS-DOS soon after the release of the C-128. But, you can still find CP/M software for download through the Internet.

C-64 and C-128 Software

The following web sites, at the time of this writing, provide C-128/64 software (much of it for free), reviews, and more links to other similar sites. These are just some of many sites:

commodore.software
commodore.ca
csdb.dk
everythingcommodore.com
commodoreserver.com
gamebase64.com
c64.com
www.breadbox64.com
8bitfiles.net
cbm8bit.com
zimmers.net/anonftp/pub/cbm/index.html
tpug.ca (order their CD)
retroisle.com/commodore/c64128/software.php

archive.org/details/Commodore_C128_TOSEC_2012_04_23
classicreload.com
protovision.games (current day game developer)
hvsc.c64.org (SID collection music)
commodore.se
vintageisthenewold.com
cbmfiles.com
loadstargallery.webs.com
istilladoremy64.chorusgrove.com
lemon64.com
tnd64.unikat.sk
megastyle.itch.io
www.psytronik.net/newsite/
www.blackcastlesoftware.com
rksoft.info
www.particles.org/particlesbbs/projects/
sites.google.com/site/h2obsession/CBM/C128
www.c64music.co.uk/
www.indieretronews.com/search/label/C128

CP/M information and software

www.classiccmp.org/cpmarchives/
www.zimmers.net/anonftp/pub/cpm/
www.particles.org/particlesbbs/projects/
www.z80.eu/c128.html
www.herne.com/cpm.htm
sites.google.com/site/h2obsession/CBM/C128/cp-m
commodore128.mirkosoft.sk/cpm.html
www.devili.iki.fi/Computers/Commodore/C128/CPM-tech/
rvbelzen.tripod.com/
pcsauro.altervista.org/CPM.PHP
www.floodgap.com/retrobits/ckb/ (use search term "cp/m")
www.seasip.info/Cpm/index.html
www.cbmfiles.com/genie/C128CPMListing.php
www.retroisle.com/commodore/c64128/Articles/c128_cpm.php
www.filegate.net/cbm/8-cpm/
www.cpm8680.com/cpmc64/cpmsys2.htm
www.cpm.z80.de/binary.html

9.2 How to get the software onto the C-128

In most cases, a vintage C-128 owner will download software using another computer and then transfer the files over to a C-128 storage device, like a floppy disk drive or an SD card reader. Files with the PRG extension are Commodore format files and, when transferred onto a floppy disk, can be run as is. Files with D64, D71, or D81 extensions will need special treatment. See next section for that discussion.

If you don't have a disk drive, a simple way to proceed is to get an SD2IEC. That way, you can easily and quickly use the newly downloaded files on your C-128. You use your other computer (Linux, Windows, etc.) with a generic SD card reader for your PC. Go onto the Internet to one of the sites mentioned in this book, or elsewhere if you have other recommendations. Download the files and save them to your SD card.

After you have downloaded onto the SD card, remove it from the PC reader and insert it into your SD2IEC. At that point, you can load and run the programs on your C-128. As mentioned earlier in this book, it is a good idea to use the Commodore file browser, which will let you navigate through the SD card's folders and files. There are several tutorials on how to use SD card readers on the C-128/64 online. Take a look on YouTube for video tutorials. TheFutureWas8Bit (tfw8b.com) has produced their own tutorial video available on YouTube for their SD2IEC. Other YouTube videos are available for similar SD devices, such as the uIEC/SD from RETRO Innovations (go4retro.com), and others. (Note: There are USB devices that act in a similar way. Not having worked with USB on the C-128, I cannot provide usage details.)

If you already have a device for going online with your C-128 (see Chapter 7 Telecommunications), you can log into a

Commodore BBS and download programs directly onto your storage device, whether a floppy disk or SD card or USB stick.

What if you don't have access to your own PC connected to the Internet? Perhaps your access to the Internet is on a shared PC in a public library where you can't download. You can still get software without downloading it. For example, if you get an SD2IEC from TheFutureWas8Bit (tfw8b.com) you can buy an SD card that has a huge number of programs on it. Also, the Toronto PET Users Group (tpug.ca), sells a CD filled with Commodore programs, including those for the 64, 128, and CP/M modes. These are just two places where you can get software for your C-128, without having to download.

9.3 How to handle Disk Images

The software that you download from the Internet will come in various file formats. PRG files are ready to load and run on your Commodore. However, most files will be in some kind of an archived format, such as D64, D71, or D81. These different disk image files refer to the disks that are designed for use with the Commodore 1541, 1571, or 1581 disk drives. In many cases, the disk image file will have been zipped, so you will download a ZIP, which, when unzipped, is extracted into one of the disk image file formats. You can unzip the files on your PC. The C-128 also has zip and unzip utility programs (see www.zimmers.net/commie/need.html).

A disk image is a single file that replicates an entire disk of data. Many commercial programs from decades ago, which were multi-file programs on a floppy disk or multiple floppies, have been converted into disk image files. So, when you see a D64, D71, or D81, this is an exact duplicate of an entire disk of files crammed into one file. For software that had more than one disk, there will be more than one disk image (Ex. file-1.d64, file-2.d64). You can run a disk image file, as is, on an SD2IEC (or a USB device). In Chapter 3.3, we discussed SD2IECs that are available with selection buttons to change from one disk image to another when running a multi-disk program, thereby switching disks.

As mentioned earlier, there are file browsers that you use to move among directories on an SD card. CBM FileBrowser (commodore.software) is widely recommended. This browser will allow you to load and run disk image files. Basically, from a menu, you find the disk image that you want to run and click on it. That moves you inside the disk image directory where you click on the program file. The browser automates the load and run commands.

You cannot run a disk image, as is, from a floppy disk drive. If you want to run disk images on your Commodore disk drive, you need to transfer the disk image onto a Commodore floppy disk, the image having been extracted into separate files in the process. There are many ways of accomplishing this. Some are more difficult to achieve than others; there is a learning curve.

There are file management programs for the 128 mode and 64 mode that can do this. CBM Command (commodoreserver.com) and DraCopy128 (commodore.software) are popular. For 64 mode, SDBrowse (csdb.dk) gets good reviews. With these utility programs, you basically select a disk image on the SD card, display the directory of files inside the disk image, and then copy all of those individual files onto the floppy disk drive. These copy programs accomplish the task and the software is free.

If you have a large number of disk images that you want to transfer to floppy disks, you might want to buy a hardware device, which would accomplish the task faster. This is a bit more complicated than just running a file copier. In general, the process involves connecting your Commodore disk drive to your PC and then moving files from the PC onto the Commodore floppy disk. You use a utility program on the PC, such as OpenCBM (opencbm.trikaliotis.net) which runs on Linux or Windows PCs. There are various hardware devices that do this. One of them is ZoomFloppy, from RETRO Innovations (go4retro.com).

Another hardware device, the WiModem (cbmstuff.com), used in conjunction with the utility programs, WIHD and WICOPY, will help to accomplish this. See Chapter 7.3.

YouTube has videos that explain how to accomplish transferring disk images onto floppy disks. Check into some of these. Also, check into the Commodore forums to see what others say about which devices and cables they recommend, and what utility programs they use.

While we are here discussing disk images, you might also want to know about a Windows-based GUI application, called DirMaster (style64.org/dirmaster). DirMaster allows you to manipulate disk images on a PC, which you later can transfer over to your Commodore data device to run on your C-128. This is a bit more advanced and offers many features for creating, editing, and doing many things with Commodore disk images.

This ends our look at handling disk images on the C-128.

9.4 Where To Look For More C-128 Information

This section provides the names of publications, user groups, and organizations that were active in 1985 (some of these are still active in 2019). The information is categorized by topic. Many of the magazines are still available in archival form from a variety of online sites, and those sites are referenced in italics with the magazine description.

Additionally, lists of current day publications, active Commodore forums, and Commodore movies/documentaries are included at the end of this section.

Fig. 9-2. Where to look for more C-128 Information

Commodore Specific Magazines from the Old Days

Ahoy!

Ahoy! was a monthly magazine which offered tutorial articles, program listings, and reviews of Commodore products. It covered the C-128, C-64, and VIC 20. You can get archives of Ahoy! online in various locations, such as commodore.ca and archive.org.

Commodore Microcomputers

This bi-monthly magazine held articles, product reviews, and program listings for the C-128, as well as other Commodore computers. This magazine was supported directly by Commodore. Archival issues are currently available online at archive.org and issuu.com.

Commodore Power Play

This was a companion bi-monthly publication put out by Commodore. It included articles, program listings, and software reviews for Commodore computers. Archival issues are currently available online at archive.org and scribd.com.

Compute!'s Gazette

Compute!'s Gazette was a monthly magazine devoted to the C-128, C-64, VIC 20, Plus/4, and C-16 computers. Compute! also had a book publishing firm which put out many fine books concerning topics of interest to Commodore computerists. Archival issues are currently available online at archive.org and commodore.ca.

RUN Magazine

RUN was a monthly magazine devoted to the C-128, C-64, Plus/4, C-16, and VIC 20. It held articles, product reviews, and program listings of interest to Commodore computer users. RUN was a good source of information for the Commodore computer user, as well as those who want to learn hints and tips about programming their computer. Archival issues are currently available online at archive.org and commodore.ca.

TPUG Magazine

TPUG was a magazine put out by the Toronto Pet Users Group. This group was the largest Commodore user's group in the world in the 1980s. The magazine was quite informative and covered all of the Commodore computers: C-64, C-128, VIC 20, PET/CBM, and SuperPET. TPUG held an annual convention in Toronto (and still does) and had a BBS which members could join. TPUG also has a library available to members which is full of public domain software. Archival issues of TPUG Magazine are currently available online at archive.org and tpug.ca. The Toronto PET Users Group is still alive and well in 2019. You can visit them online at tpug.ca.

Transactor

Transactor was another magazine published in Canada for Commodore computerists. It covered many Commodore computers: PET, CBM, VIC 20, C-64, and C-128. This was a good source of information on the more technical aspects of computing and includes many programming aids and utilities. Archival issues are currently available online at archive.org and csbruce.com/cbm/transactor.

ZZap!64 Magazine

Zzap!64 was a computer games magazine covering games on Commodore computers, especially the C-64. It was published in the U.K. by Newsfield Publications Ltd and later by Europress Impact. The magazine was published from 1985 to 1994. Archival issues are currently available online at archive.org.

CP/M Resources

User's Guide: The Magazine for CP/M and MS-DOS Computer Users (TUG Inc.)

The User's Guide was published six times a year and was a top notch source of hands-on information for CP/M users. It held in-depth tutorials on how to handle various CP/M software and also included information on how to obtain and use public domain software.

First Osborne Group

FOG was a user group for CP/M users. The systems covered include the Osborne 1, Osborne Executive 1, all models of the Morrow MicroDecision, the Zorba, and all models of KayPro. Many of these computers were compatible with CP/M 3 in the Commodore 128. FOG had a magazine which it sent out to members, called Foghorn.

Micro/Systems Journal

The Micro/Systems Journal held technical information for programmers and software and hardware tutorials, reviews, and public domain software information. It covered many microcomputers, some of which include CP/M based machines. This journal is available through various libraries. See www.worldcat.org for a list of some libraries where this is available.

CP/M Software Finder (Digital Research)

The CP/M Software Finder was a listing of all of the CP/M software available commercially. It included names and descriptions of software as well as what type of CP/M computers the software worked on. The CP/M Software Finder was categorized by topic so that you could easily find what was available. This is available in book form through various libraries. See www.worldcat.org for a list of some libraries where this is available.

Digital Research

CP/M - The First PC Operating System

This is a web site devoted to telling the story about the origins of CP/M and its developer, Dr. Gary A. Kildall. Currently available at www.digitalresearch.biz.

Education and Computing

MECC

Minnesota Educational Computing Consortium (MECC) provided software for colleges and schools. MECC provided help in development and distribution of computer software, in-service training for educators, assistance through newsletters, and management information services. See mecc.co for current information.

Family Guide To Educational Software (L.F. Garlinghouse Co. Inc.)

The Family Guide To Educational Software provided a quarterly magazine which held descriptions of many educational programs for all levels of home users. In 1985, you could order software from Garlinghouse at discount prices.

T.H.E. Journal (Information Synergy, Inc.)

The T.H.E. Journal holds articles written by professional educators on topics relating to computers in education. In 1985, it was released ten times a year. This journal is a good source for information about new product releases and for reading the opinions of professionals who are using computers in teaching. Currently active and available online at thejournal.com.

Educational Resources for Microcomputers (The Software Directory)

The Educational Resources for Microcomputers Software Directory is a compilation of abstracts from the Microsearch Database. It covers educational software which has been abstracted for that online database. Sources are from product literature and review articles from magazines. It also includes a listing of all software manufacturers cited in the book. This is available in book form through various libraries. See www.worldcat.org for a list of libraries where this is available.

Computers in Education (Moorshead Publications Ltd.)

Computers in Education was published ten times a year and held articles written by educators using computers in their classrooms. It also included educational software reviews and software recommendations.

Telecommunications

Tele Journal (Wayne Green Enterprises)

The Tele Journal was a magazine devoted to the small business user and telecommunications. It included articles about businesses that were using telecommunications as part of their operation and also product reviews.

<u>Link-Up (Learned Information, Inc.)</u>

Link-Up was a monthly tabloid devoted to online and videotex uses of microcomputers for business, home, and schools. See www.infotoday.com/lu/lunew.htm for information about archival issues of Link-Up.

Present Day Commodore News and Publications

There are present day publications for Commodore computers that include news and information. Provided below are links (as of January, 2019) to resources about recent Commodore magazines, disk magazines, podcasts, videos, new hardware, and new software for the C-128/C-64 and other Commodore computers.

Commodore News Page

commodore-news.com/news/magazine/1/en

www.richardlagendijk.nl/cnp/home/index/1/en

Commodore Free Magazine

www.commodorefree.com

Scene World Magazine

sceneworld.org/

RESET Magazine

reset.cbm8bit.com/

Komoda & Amiga Plus Magazine

ka-plus.pl/en/main/

The Retrogaming Times

www.classicplastic.net/trt/

Kilobyte Magazine

issuu.com/kilobytemagazine

Freeze64 Magazine

freeze64.com/

Attitude Magazine

www.cactus.jawnet.pl/attitude/

CSDb - The C64 Scene Database

csdb.dk

This site posts a wide variety of disk magazines

for Commodore computers.

Commodore Forums

Commodore Forums (message boards) are valuable resources for learning more about your C-128. You can read the Q&As and discussions of others on these forums, and you can post your own questions and receive answers from other Commodore users who have experience with your topic. You will also find a lot of forum activity in Commodore Bulletin Board systems (see Chapter 7 to review the information about BBSs). Companies that produce and sell products for the C-128 and C-64 often have their own forums, too, where you can ask questions about their products.

Here is a short list in alphabetical order of some of the Commodore Forums on the web that you might want to visit. In most Commodore forums, there will be an area for other 8-bit computers or C-128 in particular.

AtariAge

atariage.com/forums/forum/172-commodore-8-bit-computers/

C128.com

c128.com/forums/forums

See also the main page, c128.com, for interesting

articles about Commodore and the C-128.

CBM8Bit (list of forums)

cbm8bit.com/weblinks/8bit/commodore

Commodore.ca

www.commodore.ca/forum/

Forum64

www.forum64.de

Lemon64

www.lemon64.com/forum/

Melon64

www.melon64.com/forum/

Toronto PET Users Group

www.tpug.ca/forums/

Movies and Documentaries

The Commodore Story (2018)

8 Bit Generation: The Commodore Wars (2017)

JACK and the MACHINE: An Interactive Documentary

Now that we are in the age of the Internet search engine, it is easy to locate information about almost any topic. Throughout this book, there are references to additional web sites and companies that deal with the C-128, C-64, and CP/M. You are encouraged to visit these sites and search for even more resources online.

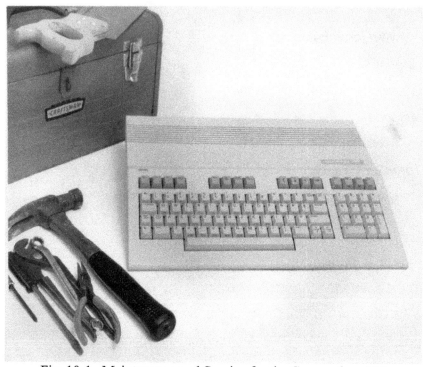

Fig. 10-1. Maintenance and Service for the Commodore 128

Chapter 10

Maintenance and Service for the Commodore 128

One of the most overlooked areas of computer use is maintenance. Many computer owners don't know what is likely to go wrong with their computer system, what components are most apt to have problems, and what to do to help postpone equipment failure. Because of this gap in their knowledge, people tend to be devastated when their equipment finally does fail and must go in for servicing or repair. This is because they often have no idea of what has caused a failure, and they don't know where to turn for advice and help.

This section was originally written for the 1985 reader, but current day C-128 users will find much of this information applicable today.

10.1   Do-It-Yourself Maintenance

Computers themselves are often described as being maintenance free because they don't have any moving parts except the keys, but once you look closely at your peripherals, you will discover that there are plenty of moving parts present in your system. Moving parts wear out, and electronic non-moving components can develop electrical problems. There is also the problem of poor air quality and other environmental factors which can damage your computer equipment.

What follows are some common preventive maintenance procedures that you can perform on a regular basis on your own equipment. An underlying requirement for maintaining your computer system is the presence of an appropriate location and environment. Chapter 3 discussed the considerations in selecting an appropriate computer work station. Many factors which were discussed there are important as preventive maintenance measures, also. Given the fact that you have already chosen a safe location for your computer and its peripherals, here are some points of concern that you should address on a regular basis.

Computer

The computer itself requires the least maintenance of any system component. Most of its important parts are protected within the casing and are non-mechanical. The only moving parts are the on-off switch and the keys on the keyboard, but there are still some important procedures that you should take care of periodically.

Always be sure that the air vents on your computer are clean. Dust is one of the prime causes of computer failure. You can keep your computer dust free with just a quick vacuuming once every few weeks. You can also purchase pressurized air which can be used for blowing dust away from tiny vent openings. It is a good idea to buy a keyboard dust cover to protect the keyboard whenever the computer is not being used.

You should make sure that your computer is positioned on a sturdy table or desk so that there is no possibility of it falling to the floor. Also, don't place your computer on a table which is subjected to vibration, such as one on which a printer is used. The constant shaking might loosen internal circuitry.

The air quality of your computer room is crucial to a healthy computer system. Smoking should not be allowed for several reasons. First of all, smoke leaves a combination of sticky film and particles which will clog up your keyboard and coat your equipment. More important is the effect of smoke on disks and cassette tapes. The magnetic surfaces of these software media can easily become damaged by particles of cigarette smoke. Cooking smoke has the same effect.

Some people ban food and liquids from computer rooms. You don't have to go overboard, especially if your computer is at home, but you should be very careful not to let liquids or food particles fall into your keyboard or your disk drive. Liquids on an electronic circuit board can mean instant break down, and even fire.

Keep the temperature between 60 and 80 degrees Fahrenheit. When room temperature gets too high, there is a greater likelihood of hardware failure. This is similar to a car which works fine on cold and warm days, but overheats on hot days. Regarding vents again, don't cover the vents on any computer equipment as these are a means for preventing internal parts from overheating. Software media will also be damaged by too low or too high temperatures.

See also Chapter 4 for more details about a safe workspace for your computer.

Electrical Safety

Be sure not to plug in or unplug any peripherals or cartridges from your computer unless it is turned off. If you will be using your computer intermittently throughout the day, just leave it on all day. This prevents the on-off switch from getting too much use and it saves wear and tear on the internal circuitry. Excessive heating and cooling of chips tends to wear them out and the expansion and contraction can damage connections.

Unplug the computer's power supply when you are finished using your computer for the day, or turn off the power strip. This will prevent the power supply from wearing out prematurely.

A stable electrical power supply is a crucial concern for your computer's safety. Power surges and power drops will cause problems. A power surge can overheat and even burn out the internal circuitry of your computer. The easiest way to prevent a power surge from reaching your computer is to buy a surge protector/power strip. You should also avoid using your equipment during a thunderstorm because the lightning can cause power surges. Never plug or unplug any computer equipment unless it is turned off. This is especially true of cartridges and modems. The result to the computer's delicate circuitry is the same as a voltage surge.

Power drops can cause loss of data from your computer's RAM memory. While this won't harm your computer, it is extremely exasperating. If you happen to be working on something important at the time, you are quite likely to lose all of the information in memory if the power to your computer suddenly drops. A power fluctuation can occur if you have your computer on the same electrical circuit as your refrigerator, air conditioner, electric tools, freezer, or water pump. Every time one of these items comes on, the electrical current to your computer might drop. You can prevent this by avoiding electrical circuits which handle appliances that cycle on and off. A loose plug or cable connector can cause the same type of power drop.

Monitor or Television

The upkeep and protection of your monitor or television is very simple. The tops of CRT monitors tend to collect junk. It is human nature to place a piece of paper or a manual on top of your monitor, using it as a supplemental table. Even with a flatscreen monitor or TV, make sure not to block any cooling vents, and don't let any foreign objects, such as food or drink, accidentally fall inside.

To keep the screen display of any monitor in good condition, always turn the brightness down when you are not actively using the monitor, or turn off the monitor. This prevents screen burn. Screen burn is when a faded copy of an image is permanently imprinted onto your screen, after long periods of displaying the same image with a bright display.

Disk Drives

There are three things you should watch out for concerning disk drives. First, you should keep your drive clear of debris which will block the air vents and cause overheating. If needed, a fan can help keep your drive cool. You can get a very small one for just the drive, or a larger one to blow air around all of your equipment. Don't immediately buy a cooling fan though; it might not be needed in your situation.

Second, you should periodically clean the disk drive head. This is not difficult and can prolong the life of your drive as well as avoid many problems with faulty disk saves and loads. Think of your disk drive as similar to an 8-track or cassette tape deck. They each have a head mechanism that presses against a moving surface in order to interpret information held on the magnetic tape or disk. After prolonged use, the head mechanism collects matter such as dust and grime which impairs the head's ability to accurately transfer information. When your disk drive starts making loading and saving mistakes, your first act should be to clean the head, not go to the computer repair man.

The 5 and 1/4 inch floppy disk drives that you will use with your C-128 will either be single sided like the 1541, or double sided like the 1571 drive. A single sided disk drive has one read-write head which reads only one side of a disk at a time. In the 1541 drive, the read-write head is on the bottom pointing upward to read the lower side of the disk. The 1571 has two read-write heads, one on the top and one on the bottom. It is not necessary to see the read-write head to clean it, so disassembly of the drive is not needed. Knowing the location of the head and what part of your cleaning disk needs to touch it is important when you try to use a universal cleaning kit with no machine-specific instructions.

In order to clean either of the Commodore floppy disk drives, you will need to purchase a 5 and 1/4 inch disk drive head cleaning kit. You don't have to use a Commodore kit; any brand will do. The cleaning kit will have several floppy disks with white material disks inside them rather than magnetic disks. There will also be a bottle of liquid cleaning fluid. To use a standard cleaning disk, pour the cleaning fluid onto the exposed white material seen through the large cut-out section. This area corresponds to the exposed elongated opening on the bottom of your disk where the read-write head touches the disk.

For 1541 drives, insert the cleaning disk with the large cut-out facing downward. For double sided drives like the 1571, you will need to pop off the removable section on the other side of the cleaning disk. Be sure that you have the cleaning fluid on both sides of the white material. Insert the cleaning disk. It is absolutely necessary for that second opening to be free in a double sided drive so that the top read-write head won't get damaged by moving over the plastic disk jacket. Once you have the disk in place, you need to activate the drive for about 30 seconds.

Some kits recommend cleaning once a week, but it actually depends upon how often you use your drive. Recently, it has been suggested that too many head cleaning sessions can wear out the head. You'll have to be your own judge as to how often you perform this self maintenance procedure. Most cleaning disks handle about 13 sessions, but this will vary according to how dirty your drive is each time you use the kit. If the white material looks dirty, throw the cleaning disk away.

Floppy disk cleaning kits for 5 1/4 inch drives are not popular in this century. You might find one on eBay. If you can't locate a cleaning kit, there are instructions on the Internet from various sources on how to accomplish this without a kit, using household materials.

The third self maintenance item concerns disk drive head alignment. Disk drives come factory aligned and ready for use. Through long usage, the read-write heads can move out of alignment, just like the front wheels on your car. Your disk drive, like your car's front wheels, will continue to function while out of alignment, but it can get worse. Your software will not load properly and your drive will work overtime to accomplish simple writes and reads. Another sure way to tell that your head is out of alignment is if your self made software loads and works but new commercial software doesn't. This happens because your disk will be synchronized with your drive, but a factory made disk, whose tracks are correctly positioned, will be out of sync with your drive.

There is no way to prevent misalignment of your disk drive heads; however, once you realize that the heads are out of line, you should get them realigned as soon as possible. You can do your own realigning, but you will need detailed instructions on how to do it. If you don't know someone who can help you out, you probably would be better off bringing your drive to a computer repair shop.

Floppy Disks

The computer programs stored on your disks tell your computer what to do. You will accumulate more and more floppy disks to hold software programs as you purchase commercial software, write your own programs, and download programs via modem from user's groups and other public domain sources.

Handle your disks carefully. They are very valuable. Always make back-ups of important disks. This way, you won't feel so bad when your working copy of your most important program crashes.

Here are some common do's and don'ts to consider:

DON'T:

- Place disks near an electromagnetic force like that produced by a monitor, disk drive, electric tools, a vacuum cleaner, or a magnet.
- Bend disks.
- Touch the magnetic surface with your fingers or any object.
- Expose disks to liquids or any other foreign substances such as dust or smoke.
- Expose disks to very high or low temperatures.
- Write on disk labels with ballpoint pens while the labels are on the disk.
- Overcrowd disks within a single box.

DO:

- Store disks in their protective paper envelopes.
- Store disks upright in a non-metallic box.
- Insert disks into the drive properly, without forcing or bending them.

Cassettes

Care of your cassettes and the Datassette is similar to that of disks and a disk drive. The same rules apply. Avoid dust, smoke, and magnetic forces. Store tapes in a protective non-metallic box, as you would disks. Keep the recorder clean. Periodically, you may need to realign the cassette recorder's heads. There is a simple procedure for doing this which requires only a small screwdriver. Ask your local Commodore user's group or computer repair shop for advice on this procedure.

Printers

In 1985, printers were very different than they are today. Many printers back then used inked ribbons and tractor feed paper with holes along each side. This type of printer required care that you won't see the need for in modern printers. This discussion pertains mostly to owners of vintage printers, yet some of it can be applied to modern printers, too.

Printers are likely to require repair before any other component in your computer system. This is because printers have the most moving parts. You should always keep your printer on a stable surface and try to keep vibration to a minimum. Be sure that the paper path is unhindered and is lined up with the printer feed mechanism.

Keep your printer clean by vacuuming it inside and out. Check for collection of dust and grime around the print head and in the air vents. Most printers do not need preventive maintenance such as oiling. About all that you can do aside from keeping it clean and free of foreign objects is to keep the paper feed unobstructed, be sure that your ribbons are in good shape, and make sure that your paper isn't too thick or too thin. Don't run any printer without a ribbon and paper in it. If you are getting paper or ribbon jams, you can untangle the mess and straighten things out fairly easily. You will also be able to handle simple repairs to the exposed parts such as a loose screw or a blown fuse.

10.2 Service

We have covered some of the more common careful handling tips and preventive maintenance measures that you should perform at regular intervals. Now, let's look at another avenue for maintenance: getting your computer equipment serviced by a professional.

In the spring of 1985, Commodore implemented a nationwide service arrangement with computer stores and electronics repair businesses. By telephoning Commodore Customer Support, you could get the names and addresses of authorized Commodore service centers in your area. By early spring of 1985, there were already two hundred RCA dealers, as well as thirteen hundred computer stores which were authorized to service your Commodore computer.

In 2019, there are repair and restoration service providers for vintage/retro computers, like the C-128. My experience was referenced in Chapter 1.2 with Ray Carlsen. There are others. Do a quick Internet search for "Commodore computer repair" and you will find a variety of service providers. It is likely that they will not be in your local area, so you will need to carefully box up your equipment and mail it off. Discuss with the service provider the best way to pack your equipment. In some cases, the postage for mailing will match or exceed the actual repair cost.

10.3 Troubleshooting

Many problems that you encounter with your computer system stem from either a mistake that you made in giving a command, a problem with the software media, or problems with loose cable connections. More often than not, the problem has not been caused by defective hardware. If your computer locks up, or refuses to continue functioning as you hoped it would, try shutting off the machine and all of its peripherals, and then start up all over again. Many times, just this simple procedure will overcome a problem.

If you are sure that your computer is set up properly and that you are giving proper loading instructions, then your disk drive might be the problem. You should clean the heads first, and if that doesn't work, bring it to your service dealer to check the head alignment.

Quite often, problems stem from loose power supply connections. If your computer goes dead, check the power supply cord to the computer and the plug into the outlet. Make sure that both are snug. The power supply has a fuse built into the bottom of it that might be blown. Checking the power supply cords and cables applies also to your monitor, disk drive, and printer. Check the power supply connections first. Often, a plug isn't inserted all the way and even the slightest vibration dislodges it.

In most cases, you shouldn't open the cases on your computer, monitor, or your disk drive. Be sure not to open up this equipment if it is still under warranty or if it is under a service contract. Both may be voided by your tampering with the insides of the machinery. Leave this for a professional. (Of course, this is a moot point for a vintage computer.)

There are other simple things that you can do to fix a problem. For example, if you are using a television set with your computer, you might not have your channel selector set correctly. There are only two channels (3 and 4) that your computer will work with. If your monitor doesn't display anything, first check to make sure that the brightness and contrast are set properly. It might just simply be a matter of turning a few knobs to bring the picture into view. If you're not getting any sound, maybe your volume knob is turned down too low. Sometimes, your picture won't come in clearly because the cable to your monitor or television is too close to an electro-magnetic field. You should not keep your disk drive or Datassette too close to your monitor because they might interfere with your display. Try repositioning cables.

If you follow the preventive maintenance procedures recommended in this chapter, the location advice presented in Chapter 4, and the directions for set up in the various manuals accompanying the computer equipment, then you will be well equipped to take care of your system and maximize its lifespan. You don't need to be a technician to keep your equipment in good working condition. Through smart care and handling, you will know when you need to turn to a professional for advice.

In addition, it is wise to gather together your own reference library of maintenance guides and books dealing with your computer, its peripherals, and the software that you use. These reference books, like the one you're reading now, can give you information that you will use over and over again. What you don't see covered in one book, you will probably find in another. You can become well informed about your C-128 by taking the time to collect several sources of information and studying them.

This ends the discussion of maintenance and service for your C-128. The following Appendices hold valuable reference materials that you will want to come back to again and again. Take a look and ...

Enjoy your Commodore 128 for many more years to come.

Fig. A-1. Commodore 128 Personal Computer

Appendix A

Glossary of Computer Terms

Access: To read, write, or update information; to read the data in order to perform a read, write, or update operation.

Acoustic modem: A modem which sends and receives data as audible tones. See Direct connect modem.

Address: A number or string of characters used to identify a particular location in memory.

Algorithm: A specific procedure which a program follows to complete a task.

Alpha numeric: Used to describe anything which may contain both numbers and letters.

Applications software: Programs used for specific tasks. Word processing is an example.

Application: Any use for a computer, often used interchangeably with program.

Array: A user definable set of values with one or more dimensions. You can identify a certain value by its position in the array. Data can be entered into and retrieved from an array by referring to its particular coordinates.

ASCII: An acronym for American Standard Code for Information Interchange. This standard allows computers which were manufactured by different companies to communicate in a standard text format.

Assembler: A program which converts source code, written in assembly language, into object code. Often assemblers are integrated with a text editor and a debugger.

Assembly language: A computer language which closely parallels machine language. Each machine language statement corresponds to an easier to remember assembly language command.

Asynchronous: A method of data I/O in which simultaneous sending and receiving is impossible.

Backup: A duplicate of computer data, used in the event that the original is destroyed.

BAM: Block Allocation Map. An area of disk space which holds the disk's name, ID, and a record of which sectors are filled.

BASIC: Beginner's All-purpose Symbolic Instruction Code. BASIC is one of the most commonly used computer languages for beginners today.

Baud: The rate at which a computer peripheral can transmit data. The term bits per second can be used interchangeably with baud.

BBS: See Bulletin board system.

Binary: A numbering system using base-2. The counting method computers use. Each digit of a binary number can be only 1 or 0.

Bit: The smallest piece of information a computer can store. A bit can be in only two states: on (1) or off (0). See byte.

Bit map: An area of RAM whose contents determine what will be displayed on a computer's screen as bit mapped graphics.

Bit mapped graphics: A type of computer graphics which deals with the computer's display on a pixel by pixel basis.

Board: 1. An abbreviation for bulletin hoard system. 2. Inside a computer, a flat piece of plastic with computer chips embedded in it. Example: a motherboard.

Boot: A process of activating some part of a computer system. It is possible to boot both hardware and software.

Buffer: An area of RAM reserved by a program for temporary data storage.

Bug: A mistake in a program which causes undesirable results. Debugging removes mistakes from programs.

Bulletin board system: A computer network system which can be accessed by other computers via modem.

Bus: A communications channel which permits a computer to talk to connected peripherals.

Byte: A number stored in a computer and composed of eight bits. A byte can represent any number from 0 to 255.

Carrier tone: The tone emitted by a computer with a modem when it is first called and trying to establish a connection.

Cartridge: A small box, containing a ROM program, which can be inserted into a special port on some computers.

Cassette drive: A peripheral which stores and retrieves programs or data on magnetic cassette.

Cell: One box on a spreadsheet's grid.

Central processing unit: The brain of a computer system which performs all arithmetic and decision making functions.

Character set: An area of memory which defines the way in which a computer will display the characters it is capable of manipulating.

Chip: A type of computer micro electronics which is etched onto a silicon wafer. An integrated circuit.

COBOL: COmmon Business Oriented Language. A computer language designed primarily for business applications.

Code: Informal term referring to a computer program's source or object code.

Compatibility: Refers to the interchangeability of computer hardware or software.

Compiler: A program which reads source code written in a computer language and outputs the machine language equivalent.

Computer: A device which manipulates information, using a CPU, memory, programs, and peripherals.

Computer language: A system of well defined syntax through which a computer can be programmed to perform a specific task.

Computer network: Any system of linked computers and/or terminals.

CP/M: Control Program for Microcomputers. CP/M is a disk operating system standard which allows a piece of software to be compatible with several different types of computers.

CPS: Characters Per Second. The rate of transmission for a computer peripheral.

CPU: Central Processing Unit. See above.

Crash: A term describing the failure of a computer system.

CRT: Cathode Ray Tube. Another way to describe the television or monitor which a computer is using for display purposes.

Cursor: A marker which is displayed on the computer's screen to indicate where the user is working.

Daisy wheel printer: A type of printer which uses a predefined set of characters, similar to an electronic typewriter. The characters inside a daisy wheel printer are arranged in a circular pattern, hence the name. See also Dot matrix printer.

Data: Information entered into the computer which the computer can manipulate, store, or display.

Database: A program designed to store and manipulate data as records with one or more fields. This data can then be sorted or recalled according to the information in any of these fields.

Data communications: Any transfer of data between computers.

Data processing: The act of entering or manipulating data with a computer.

Debugger: A program which helps a programmer to find and fix errors in his/her program.

Decimal: A numbering system using base-10.

Dedicated: A computer system set up to do one particular task, like a dedicated word processor.

Default: The state of any user-alterable condition before a user changes it.

Direct connect modem: A modem which transmits and receives data as electrical pulses. See Acoustic modem.

Directory: 1. An area of disk space reserved for the names, lengths, and types of the files on a disk. 2. A display of the information stored on the disk directory.

Disk Drive: A peripheral which stores and retrieves programs or data on magnetic diskettes.

Diskette: A disk composed of magnetic material similar to that of audio cassettes. Diskettes, known also as disks, are permanently enclosed in a disk jacket to protect them from dust and handling.

Display: 1. To make visible on the computer screen. 2. What is visible on the computer screen.

Documentation: Information on the correct usage of a program.

DOS: Disk Operating System. The set of routines which handle the housekeeping functions on a disk system. For example, this would include writing and erasing files.

Dot matrix printer: A type of printer which forms its characters from a matrix of dots, called the print head. Many dot matrix printers can print pictures as well as text. See Daisy wheel printer.

Double density: A type of disk format in which each sector can store 256 bytes of data. See Single density.

Down: Used in reference to a system which has crashed.

Download: To accept information over the modem from another computer.

Duplex: The transmission ability of a modem. Full duplex modems can send and receive simultaneously; half duplex modems can't.

Editor: A program which allows a user to produce and alter data on the computer.

Electronic mail: A computer-written message left by a person who calls a BBS. Electronic mail is usually private and meant for only one person to read; however, one can send batch e-mail to many recipients at one time.

Emulator: A program which allows a computer or peripheral to behave like a different kind of computer or peripheral.

Ergonomics: A branch of technology used in the design of machines, operations, and environments to match human abilities and limitations. The design of computer equipment which contributes to the physical comfort of people.

Error: A mistake while a program is being executed. Errors are usually caused by incorrect input or faulty programming.

Execute: To start a program.

Expansion: The process of acquiring additional peripherals or memory for a computer.

Field: One component of a record in a database, containing specific information on one particular characteristic of that record.

File: An area of storage, either mass storage or memory, which is reserved for specific data. Files are identified by file names.

Floppy disk: The most common type of diskette for information storage. Floppy disks are flexible and should be handled with care to prevent damage.

Flow chart: A graphic representation of the way a program executes. Specific symbols are used to represent input, output, decisions, etc.

Format: 1. A DOS function which prepares a disk for use by a specific disk drive and computer. 2. A specific way in which data is stored or displayed.

FORTRAN: FORmula TRANslation. A computer language designed for specific use in scientific applications.

Friction feed: A method to advance paper through a printer using a friction roller. This is the method employed by conventional typewriters, as well. See Tractor feed.

Function key: A key on a computer whose usage may determined by a program.

Game port: A connection between a joystick and a computer.

Garbage collection: An operation which frees RAM which was hoarded by a computer's inefficient string handling system. Garbage collection can happen in the middle of a program and is characterized by a sudden halt of all other computer functions.

Glitch: A sudden halt in program execution which is often the result of a bug.

Graphics: 1. Pictures displayed on a computer screen. 2. Anything displayed on a computer screen.

Hacker: 1. A person who programs for the shear joy of doing so, not always trying to produce something useful. 2. One who attempts to illegally gain access to a computer system, via modem.

Hardcopy: Computer output recorded on paper.

Hard disk drive: A disk drive which uses a rigid fixed disk rather than a removable floppy disk. Hard disk drives have much greater capacity and speed than other disk drives.

Hardware: A computer and its peripherals.

Head: The component of a storage peripheral which physically reads or writes data to the storage medium.

High level: Used in reference to computer languages. Generally, the higher the level of a language, the easier it is to program in. See Low level.

Icon: A small, cryptic symbol displayed on a computer screen to indicate a choice available to the user. Choices offered by icons are selected with a cursor.

Input: Data which is supplied to a program during its execution.

Instruction: A statement in a program which tells the computer to perform a specific task.

Integrated: Any part of a computer system which was formed by combining other systems, each of which could function alone.

Integrated software: Programs which share data and general command structures.

Interface: A piece of computer equipment which allows a peripheral to be connected to a computer.

Interrupt: A routine which, if certain predefined conditions are met, can take control of the computer system away from another routine.

I/O: Input/Output.

I/O port: A place on a computer where peripherals may be connected.

Joystick: A type of peripheral which allows a user to point by pushing a stick in the desired direction. A game control device.

K: Kilobyte.

Kilobyte: A measure of storage capacity. A kilobyte actually represents 1024 bytes, rather than the more obvious 1000.

Language: See Computer language.

Light pen: An input device; a peripheral resembling an ordinary pen. When a light pen is touched to a computer's screen, that location can be determined by the computer.

Load: The process of entering a program or data into a computer from a mass storage device.

Low level: Used in reference to computer languages. The lower the level of a program, the closer it resembles machine language and the harder it is for people to understand it. See High level.

Machine language: The language understood by all computers. Machine language statements are represented by binary numbers.

Mass storage: One of several types of peripherals such as a disk drive which can store data while a computer is off.

Megabyte: A million (1024*1024) bytes. Actually, it is 1,048,576 bytes.

Memory: The storage within a computer. Memory holds either programs or data. See RAM and ROM.

Menu: A list of options which is displayed by a program, waiting for a user to input his/her choice from them.

Microprocessor: A central processing unit (CPU).

Modem: MOdulator DEModulator. A peripheral which allows two computers to communicate with each other.

Monitor: A peripheral on which a computer can display data. Monitors are similar to televisions, but usually have a higher resolution.

Monochrome monitor: A display device which is only capable of displaying data in one color (usually green or amber). Monochrome monitors typically have a higher resolution than color monitors.

Mouse: A peripheral which is rolled on a flat surface and used to control a cursor.

Multitasking: The process of having more than one program executing simultaneously in a computer.

Network: See Computer network.

Object code: A program written in machine language.

Online: Used to describe anything which a user does on a terminal connected to another computer.

Operating system: The program which performs the housekeeping functions in a computer. The operating system is always running and does such things as displaying information on the screen, checking to see if any keys are pressed, etc.

OS: Operating System.

Output: Data produced by a program.

Paddle: A peripheral, resembling a knob, whose position can be read by a computer.

Page: A group of 256 consecutive bytes of memory. The first 256 bytes of a computer's memory are called Page Zero, and each successive 256 bytes are named similarly in ascending order.

Parallel I/O: A method of data transmission which allows more than one bit to be sent simultaneously. Commonly used to communicate with printers. See Serial I/O.

Parallel transmission: The act of sending data 8 bits at a time.

PC: Personal Computer.

Peripheral: Any device which can send to and/or receive data from a computer.

Personal computer: A computer which was designed primarily to increase personal productivity. Personal computers are generally less expensive and less powerful than larger business machines.

Pirate: One who gives or receives illegal copies of programs.

Pixel: The smallest area which a computer screen is capable of displaying. Pixels are the fundamental building blocks from which all graphics are formed.

Plotter: A peripheral, similar to a printer. Plotters are capable of much greater detail because they produce their images by actually drawing on the paper with pens.

Port: See I/O port.

Power supply: The source of energy by which a computer functions.

Printer: A peripheral which allows text, and sometimes graphics, to be put on paper.

Processor: See Microprocessor.

Program: A list of instructions telling the computer what to do, written using a computer language, which can be executed to perform a specific function.

Public domain: A type of program which is available to the public, free of charge.

RAM: Random Access Memory. Memory in which data can be stored and altered. Data stored in RAM is lost if the computer's power is turned off. See ROM.

Read: 1. The process of entering data into a computer from a peripheral. 2. The process of determining the contents of a memory location.

Recursion: The concept of a routine actually executing itself over and over.

Register: A location in memory which holds a specific piece of data. Most registers are updated by the operating system.

Resolution: The degree of accuracy with which something is displayed on a video monitor. Higher resolution allows finer details to be depicted. Lower resolution tends to be coarser and more blocky.

RF Modulator: Takes a computer's video signal and changes it to a form which a television set can receive.

ROM: Read Only Memory. Memory which is preprogrammed and unchangeable by the user. ROM remains intact, even with loss of power. See RAM.

Routine: A set of instructions designed to perform a specific task. All programs are routines; however, not all routines are programs.

Run: The process of starting a program.

Scan line: The thinnest horizontal line a television or monitor is capable of displaying.

Scrolling: A programming trick which makes the display screen behave like a window onto a larger screen. While scrolling, data which disappears off of a screen edge is replaced by new data on the opposite edge. Scrolling can be horizontal (data appears to move right or left) or vertical (data appears to move up or down).

Sector: The smallest physical part of a formatted disk.

Serial I/O: A method of data transmission which only allows one bit to be sent at a time. See Parallel I/O.

Sequential file: A collection of data which must be accessed in order. A sequential file is analogous to a book in which a person would have to read pages 1-37 in order to get to page 38.

SID: Sound Interface Device. The chip used to synthesize sound in the Commodore 64 and Commodore 128 computers.

Single density: A type of disk format in which each sector can hold 128 bytes of data. See Double density.

Software: Any computer program.

Source code: Any computer program not written in machine language.

Spreadsheet: A program which allows data to be entered, manipulated, and calculated on a grid of columns and rows.

Sprite: A graphic object which can be displayed and moved on a screen without affecting any graphics or text already being displayed.

Storage: Memory or mass storage devices.

String: A group of characters which can be manipulated as a single piece of data.

Structured programming: The concept of breaking a large programming task into several smaller routines and then writing one routine to control the interaction among all of the others.

Subroutine: A routine which is built into a larger program and performs a specific task.

Synchronous: Sending and receiving data simultaneously.

Syntax: The grammatical rules with which a program must conform in order to be valid. A program will not execute with improper syntax.

SYSOP: SYStem OPerator. The person responsible for the upkeep of part or all of a bulletin board system.

System: A computer, peripherals, and software.

Telecommunications: The facet of computing which deals with the sending and receiving data via the telephone lines.

Terminal: A keyboard which is hooked up to another computer system.

Timesharing system: A computer which allows more than one person to use its facilities simultaneously, via more than one terminal.

Touch tablet: A peripheral, with a flat surface, which can send the position of a stylus being pressed on it to the computer.

Tractor feed: A method of advancing paper through a printer which employs the use of sprockets and holes along the edge of the paper. See Friction feed.

Turtle graphics: A method of producing graphics which uses a cursor, called a turtle, that is capable of moving in relative angles and distances.

Up: A computer system which is functioning.

VIC: Video Interface Controller. The chip used to display graphics on the Commodore 64 and Commodore 128.

Video modulator: An interface which allows a computer to display on an ordinary television set.

Word processor: A program used to edit text. Word processors allow the composition phase of writing to take place before dedicating the text to paper.

Word wrap: A feature in some programs which will move an entire word being typed down a line if it would otherwise have to be broken up upon reaching the right margin.

Wraparound: A feature which allows a cursor which is moved off of one edge of the screen to appear on the opposite side of the screen.

Write: The process of outputting data onto a mass storage device.

Write protect notch: A notch on diskettes and cassettes which makes it impossible to write to them, thus avoiding accidental erasure.

Appendix B

128 Mode Screen Editing

Press and release the ESC key. Then press the key listed.

Insert and Delete:

ESC A	Turn on automatic insert mode.
ESC O	Turn off automatic insert mode.
ESC D	Delete 1i n e.
ESC I	Insert line.
ESC C	Cancel quote and insert mode.

Erase:

ESC Q	Erase to end of line.
ESC P	Erase to start of line.
ESC @	Erase to end of screen.

Cursor Control:

ESC J	Move to start of line.
ESC K	Move to end of line.
ESC E	Non-flashing cursor.
ESC F	Flashing cursor.

Tabs:

ESC Y	Set tab (8 spaces) stops.
ESC Z	Clear tab stops.

Scrolling:

ESC L	Turn on scrolling.
ESC M	Turn off scrolling.
ESC V	Scroll up one line.
ESC W	Scroll down one line.

Bell:

ESC G	Turn on bell.
ESC H	Turn off bell.

Windowing:

ESC B   Set bottom right corner of screen window.
ESC T   Set top left corner of screen window.

40/80 Column Control:

ESC X   Switch between 40 and 80 columns.

80 Column Mode Only:

ESC U   Underlined cursor.
ESC S   Block cursor.
ESC R   Reverse video screen.
ESC N   Normal video screen.

Control Codes

Press CTRL and key listed simultaneously.

CTRL B   Underline (80 column).
CTRL G   Bell.
CTRL I   Move cursor to next tab setting.
CTRL J   Line feed.
CTRL K   Turn on character set change.
CTRL L   Turn off character set change.
CTRL M   Carriage return and line feed. Enter a line of BASIC.
CTRL N   Set lowercase character set.
CTRL O   Turn on flash (80 column).
CTRL Q   Cursor down one line.
CTRL 9   Characters printed in reverse field.
CTRL T   Delete last character.
CTRL X   Tab set and clear.
CTRL [Send an Escape character.
CTRL]   Move cursor one column right.
CTRL ;   Move cursor one column right.
CTRL R   Turn on reverse field display.
CTRL 0   End reverse field display.

CTRL 1   Character color black.
CTRL 2   Character color white.
CTRL E   Character color white.
CTRL 3   Set character color to red (40), dark red (80).
CTRL £   Set character color to red (40), dark red (80).

CTRL 4	Character color cyan (40), light cyan (80).
CTRL 5	Character color purple (40), light purple (80).
CTRL 6	Character color green (40), dark green (80).
CTRL ↑	Character color green (40), dark green (80).
CTRL 7	Character color blue (40), dark blue (80).
CTRL =	Character color blue (40), dark blue (80).
CTRL 8	Character color yellow (40), light yellow (80).

128 Mode Commodore Key (C=) Screen Codes

Press Commodore key and key listed simultaneously.

C= 1	orange (40), dark purple (80)
C= 2	brown (40), dark yellow (80)
C= 3	light red (40/80)
C= 4	dark gray (40), dark cyan (80)
C= 5	medium gray (40/80)
C= 6	light green (40/80)
C= 7	light blue (40/80)
C= 8	light gray (40/80)

C= Shift   Toggles upper/lower-case character set (displays letters and characters on top of keys); and upper-case graphic display character set (displays capital letters and graphics symbols on front face of keys).

C=   During power up, press C= to boot up into 64 mode.

C= [Key with Graphics Symbol]
    Displays graphic symbol on the Left front of a key. Active in either character set.

Shift [Key with Graphics Symbol]
    Displays graphic symbol on the Right front of a key. Can only display right side graphic when keyboard is in upper-case/graphics character set.

128 Mode Keyboard Character Sets

There are two character sets:
1. upper-case letters and graphic characters.
2. upper-and lower-case letters.

In 80-column mode, both characters sets are available at the same time, allowing for 512 different characters. In 40-column mode, only one character set at a time may be used.

128 Mode Preprogrammed Function Keys

F1	GRAPHIC
F2	DLOAD"
F3	DIRECTORY
F4	SCNCLR
F5	DSAVE"
F6	RUN
F7	LIST
F8	MONITOR

Appendix C

C-128 CP/M 3 Editing Control Codes

CTRL A	Move cursor one character left.
CTRL B	Move cursor to beginning of command line, without affecting the contents of the line. If cursor is at beginning, this will move cursor to the end.
CTRL E	Forces physical carriage return but without sending command line to CP/M 3. Moves cursor to beginning of next line without erasing previous input.
CTRL F	Move cursor one character right.
CTRL G	Delete character under cursor. Cursor does not move. Characters to right of cursor move left one column.
CTRL H	Delete character to left of cursor. Moves cursor left one column. Characters to the right move one column left.
CTRL I	Move cursor to next tab stop. Every 8 columns. Same as pressing TAB.
CTRL J	Send command line to CP/M 3. Return cursor to beginning of a new line. Same as RETURN or CTRL M.
CTRL K	Delete to end of line from cursor.
CTRL M	Send command line to CP/M 3. Return cursor to beginning of a new line. Same as RETURN or CTRL J.
CTRL Q	Restart scrolling screen display.
CTRL R	Places # character at current cursor position and retypes the characters to the left of the cursor on a new line.
CTRL S	Halt scrolling screen display.
CTRL U	Updates the command line buffer to contain the characters to the left of the cursor. Places # character at current cursor position. Moves cursor to next line. Can use CTRL W to recall characters that were to the left of the cursor when you pressed CTRL U.
CTRL W	Recall and display previously entered command line at the operating system level and within a

running program, when CTRL W is the first
character typed after the prompt.
CTRL J, CTRL M, CTRL U, and RETURN define
the command line you can recall. If command
line contains characters, CTRL W moves cursor to
end of command line. If you press RETURN,
CP/M 3 executes the recalled command.

CTRL X   Erases all characters left of cursor and moves cursor
             to beginning of current line. Saves any characters
             to right of cursor.

CTRL Z   Home the cursor and clear screen.

Use CTRL C to terminate a running program.

CP/M 3 Commands

There are two types of commands in CP/M 3. These are provided on disk with the C-128.

1. Built-in commands: These identify programs in memory. There are six. Built-in commands are entered into the computer's memory when CP/M 3 is loaded.

2. Transient utility commands: These identify program files on disk. They are provided on the C-128 CP/M disks. You can add more transient utility commands.

List of Built-in CP/M Commands:

DIR	Displays filenames of all files in the directory, except for SYS (system).
DIRSYS	Displays filenames of files marked with the SYS attribute.
ERASE	Erases a filename from the disk directory and releases storage space of that file.
RENAME	Renames a disk file.
TYPE	Displays the contents of an ASCII (text) file.
USER	Changes to a different user number.

List of Transient CP/M Commands:

COPYSYS	Creates a new boot disk.
DATE	Sets or displays date and time.
DEVICE	Assigns logical CP/M devices to one or more physical devices, changes device driver protocol and baud rates, or sets console screen size.
DIR	Displays a directory with files and their characteristics.
DUMP	Displays a file in ASCII and hexadecimal format.
ED	Creates and changes ASCII files.
ERASE	Used for wildcard erase.
GET	Temporarily gets console input from a disk file rather than keyboard.
HELP	Displays information on how to use CP/M 3 commands.
INITDIR	Initializes a disk directory to allow time and date stamping.

PIP	Copies files and combines files.
PUT	Temporarily directs printer or console output to a disk file.
RENAME	Changes the name of a file, or a group of files using wildcard characters.
SET	Sets file options including disk labels, file attributes, type of time and date stamping and password protection.
SETDEF	Sets system options including the drive search chain.
SHOW	Displays disk and drive statistics.
SUBMIT	Automatically executes multiple commands.
TYPE	Display contents of text file (or group of files, if wildcard characters are used) on screen (and printer if desired).

Appendix D

64 Mode Screen Editing Codes

64 Mode Control Key Codes

CTRL M	Send carriage return and line feed. (Enter a line of BASIC.)
CTRL N	Activate lower case mode.
CTRL 9	Activate reversed character field.
CTRL 0	Terminate reversed character set.
CTRL R	(same)
CTRL S	Home the cursor.
CTRL T	Delete last character typed.
CTRL]	Move cursor one character right.
CTRL H	Disable character set.
CTRL I	Enable character set.
CTRL Q	Move cursor down one row.
CTRL 1	Character color black.
CTRL 2	Character color white.
CTRL E	Character color white.
CTRL 3	Character color red.
CTRL £	Character color red.
CTRL 4	Character color cyan.
CTRL 5	Character color purple.
CTRL 6	Character color green.
CTRL ↑	Character color green.
CTRL 7	Character color blue.
CTRL 8	Character color yellow.

64 Mode Commodore Key (C=) Codes

C= 1	Character color orange.
C= 2	Character color brown.
C= 3	Character color light red.
C=4	Character color gray 1.
C=5	Character color gray 2.
C=6	Character color light green.
C=7	Character color light blue.

C=8	Character color gray 3.
C= Shift	To change between character sets: upper-case/graphic character set; and upper/lower-case character set. The 64 mode has the same two character sets as the 128 mode.
C=	During power up, press C= to boot up into 64 mode.

Appendix E

BASIC 7.0 Glossary

The following glossary includes all of the C-128's BASIC commands, statements, functions, and reserved variables. Among these are the BASIC 2.0 commands from the 64 mode and the BASIC 7.0 commands of the 128 mode.

Each word is described and illustrated either with the actual syntax (form to follow), an example (in immediate mode or in programming mode), or both. Some parameters are optional within the syntax of certain terms. Optional parameters are placed within brackets[ ]. In places, there are two options that can be used: these are placed within < >.

If you are trying to learn BASIC, you will find typing in the programming examples helpful. For example, throughout this glossary, the graphics commands (BOX, CHAR, CIRCLE, COLOR, DRAW, GRAPHIC, and PAINT) hold programming lines (such as 5, 10, 20, etc.) which can be combined into a useful demo program. Abbreviations for each term are in brackets directly following the term.

ABS [A Shift B]
A numeric function which returns the absolute value of a number. All negative numbers are translated into positive.

```
Syntax:   ABS(X)

Example:  PRINT ABS(-3.587)
          3.587
```

AND [A Shift N]
This is a logical operator which lets the computer calculate the truth of several logical expressions. AND also is used to turn off selected bits.

```
Example:  IF X<10 AND X>5 THEN GOTO 100
```

APPEND [A Shift P]

A command which opens an existing sequential file on disk and sets the
pointer at the end of the file so that subsequent PRINT# (write)
statements will append new data to the end of the old file.

```
Syntax:    APPEND #Logical file number, "FILENAME", [Ddrive
           number] [<ON, >Udevice number]

Examples: APPEND #8, "SAMPLE FILE"
```

This prepares SAMPLE FILE for receiving new data.

```
           APPEND #1, "ANOTHER FILE", D0, U9
```

This prepares ANOTHER FILE on drive 0, device 9 for receiving
additional data.

ASC [A Shift S]
This numeric function returns the Commodore ASCII value (0-255) of
the first character of a string.

```
Syntax:    ASC (N$)

Example:   N$="RUN"
           PRINT ASC (N$)
           82
```

ATN [A Shift T]
This numeric function returns an angle (measured in radians) which has
the tangent (N).

```
Syntax:    ATN (N)

Example:   N=9
           PRINT ATN (N)
           1. 46013911
```

AUTO [A Shift U]

This command turns on and off automatic line numbering. After
entering a line of BASIC, press Return and the next line number will be
displayed.

Syntax: AUTO [Line#]

Example: AUTO 10

This sets the program's line numbers in increments of 10, starting at the first line number that you type in for your program.

          AUTO

Without a number, AUTO turns off the line numbering feature.

BACKUP [BA Shift C]

Used with a dual disk drive system, this command will copy the entire contents of one disk to another.

Syntax: BACKUP D Source drive TO D Destination
           drive[<ON, >Udevice]

Example: BACKUP D0 to D1

This copies all files from the disk in drive 0 onto the disk in drive 1. For use on dual drive unit 8.

          BACKUP D0 to D1,U9

Same as above, but for use on dual drive unit 9

BANK [B Shift A]

This statement designates one of sixteen memory banks within the C-128. To view a particular bank in memory using the built-in monitor, type BANK N (0-15) from within BASIC and then enter the Monitor. See the Programmer's Reference Guide for detailed information.

Syntax: BANK number

BEGIN/BEND [B Shift E/BE Shift N]
This is a conditional statement which is structured to allow for including several programming statements.

Example: 5 INPUT Y
          10 IF Y=5 THEN BEGIN:PRINT "Y IS 5."

```
20 PRINT "BECAUSE Y IS 5, THE STATEMENTS UNTIL
BEND WILL BE EXECUTED."
30 BEND:PRINT "THE BEGIN/BEND STRUCTURE HAS BEEN
FULFILLED." :GOTO 100
40 PRINT "Y DID NOT EQUAL 5, SO THE PROGRAM
BRANCHED AROUND THE BEGIN/BEND STRUCTURE.":GOTO
100
100 PRINT "THE END OF THIS SAMPLE."
```

BLOAD [B Shift L]

This command loads a binary file (program or data) into a specified location in memory. The binary file is a file which has been previously saved from the machine language monitor or from within BASIC using

BSAVE.

```
Syntax:    BLOAD "FILENAME"[,Ddrive number][,Udevice number]
           [,Bbank number][,Pstart address]
Example:   BLOAD "SPRITE",D0,U9,B1,P4096
```

This loads the data for SPRITE from drive 0, unit 9, into BANK 1 at the starting location of 4096 in memory.

BOOT [B Shift O]

This command loads and executes a machine language program from disk, beginning at the predefined starting address.

```
Syntax:    BOOT "FILENAME"[ ,Ddrive number] [<ON, >Udevice
           number]
```

```
Example:   BOOT
```

This will search for an executable machine language program on drive 0, unit 8. Then it will load and run that program automatically.

```
           BOOT "MUSIC SAMPLE",D1,U9
```

This will load and run MUSIC SAMPLE from drive 1 on unit 9.

BOX [none]

This graphics statement is used for drawing any sized rectangle or a filled polygon.

```
Syntax:    BOX[Color source] ,X1 ,Y1[ ,X2,Y2] [ ,Angle]
           [ ,Paint]
```

Color source can be 0-3.
(0=background/1=foreground/2=multicolor 1/3=multicolor 2)
X1 and Y1 are the top left coordinates.
X2 and Y2 are the bottom right coordinates. Angle is the amount of rotation of the object in degrees, clockwise. This is based on the center point of the rectangle. Paint is used to designate whether to fill the shape in (1) or leave it empty (0).

```
Example:   20 BOX 1, 25, 25, 100, 100
```

This draws an unfilled rectangle. See also the command GRAPHIC, which is used with BOX and other graphics statements.

BSAVE [B Shift 9]

Similar to BLOAD, but BSAVE is used for saving binary files to disk. You specify the starting and the ending addresses in memory when using the BSAVE command.

```
Syntax:    BSAVE "FILENAME"[,Ddrive number] [,Udevice
           number] [,Bbank number] ,Pstart addressToPending
           address
```

```
Example:   BSAVE "SPRITE", B0, P3584 TO P4096
```

BUMP [B Shift U]

This function determines which sprites have collided since the last check.

```
Syntax:    BUMP (N)
```

N is a number between 0 and 7, corresponding to sprites 1 through 8.

CATALOG [C Shift A]

This command will read and display the disk directory without disturbing any programs in memory.

Syntax: CATALOG [Ddrive number] [<ON, >Udevice number]
           [,wildcard string]

Example: CATALOG

Displays the disk directory of default drive 0 on device 8.

CHAR [CH Shift A]

This statement displays a character on screen, whether in bit mapped mode or in text mode.

Syntax: CHAR[Color source] ,X,Y[,"STRING"] [,Reverse
           flag] Reverse flag: 0=off/1=on

Example: 30 CHAR 0,2,20,"VINTAGE C-128 HANDBOOK",1

This will print the words "VINTAGE C-128 HANDBOOK" at column 2, row 20 with a reversed background.

CHR$ [C Shift H]

This string function returns the string character of a Commodore ASCII code number.

Syntax: CHR$(X)

Example: PRINT CHR$(74)
                J

CIRCLE [C Shift I]

This statement is used for drawing circles, ellipses, arcs, triangles, octagons, and other polygons.

Syntax: CIRCLE[Color source],X,Y[,XR][,YR] [,SA][,EA)
           [,Angle][,Inc]

262

(See BOX for description of color source.)
X,Y is the center point of the circle. XR,YR are radii. SA is the starting angle. EA is the ending arc angle. Angle is the rotation in degrees clockwise. Inc is the increment in degrees between line segments.

```
Example:   40 CIRCLE 1, 150, 105, 55, 10
           50 CIRCLE 1, 75, 45, 25, 18
```

CLOSE [CL Shift O]

This statement closes a file which was opened with OPEN or DOPEN.

```
Example:   CLOSE 15
```

This closes file number 15.

CLR [C Shift L]

This statement clears the variables in memory while leaving a program untouched.

```
Example:   CLR
```

CMD [C Shift M]

This command redirects screen output to another device, such as a disk drive or a printer.

```
Example:   OPEN 4, 4
           CMD4:LIST
           PRINT# 4
           CLOSE4
```

This redirects output to the printer while a program listing is made.

COLLECT [COLL Shift E]

This command frees up disk space that has been allocated to improperly closed files. It also deletes references to those files from the directory.

```
Syntax:    COLLECT [Ddrive number] [<ON, >Udevice]
```

263

Example: COLLECT DO

COLLISION [COL Shift L]

This statement detects sprite collisions and specifies an action to be taken subsequent to that collision. Usually, the action is a branch to a predefined subroutine.

Syntax: COLLISION type[,statement]

Types: 1=sprite-to-sprite/2=sprite-to-display/3=light pen(40-column mode)

Statement: the line number of a subroutine in BASIC

Example: COLLISION 1,500

Sprite-to-sprite collision at line number 500

COLOR [COL Shift O]

This statement assigns colors to one of the seven screen color areas on the C-128. Sixteen different colors can be used.

Syntax: COLOR Source number,Color number
Sources #s are:
            0= 40 column background
            1= 40 column foreground
            2= multicolor 1
            3= multicolor 2
            4= 40 column border
            5= character color in 40/80 columns
            6= 80 column background.
Colors are 1 to 16.

Example: 5 COLOR 0,5

This will color the background purple, in 40 column mode.

CONCAT [C Shift O]

This command merges, or concatenates, two sequential data files which already exist on disk.

```
Syntax:    CONCAT "Second file"[ ,Ddrive number] TO "First
           file"[ ,Ddrive number] [<ON,>Udevice number]
```

```
Example:   CONCAT "FILE 2",D0 TO "FILE 1",D1
```

This will merge files 1 and 2, placing FILE 2 at the end of FILE 1, while retaining the FILE 1 name.

CONT [64:C Shift O/128:none]

This command restarts program execution after it has been halted by STOP or END and resumes where the break occurred.

```
Example:   CONT
```

COPY [CO Shift P]

This command copies a single file or all files from one disk to another. It is also used in single drive systems for making a copy on to the same disk, but under a different name.

```
Syntax:    COPY [Ddrive number, ]"Source filename" TO
           [Ddrive number, ]"Destination filename" [<ON,
           >Udevice number]
```

```
Example:   COPY D0,"Source file" TO D1, "Destination file"
```

This will copy the Source file on the disk in drive 0 onto the disk in drive 1, and rename the file as Destination file.

COS [none]

This function returns the cosine for an angle specified in radians.

```
Example:   PRINT COS(N)
```

DATA [D Shift A]

A statement which defines the data to be input into memory by a READ statement. Numbers and words can be placed in a DATA statement. All items must be separated by commas. Words must be placed within quotation marks. DATA statements can be located anywhere in a BASIC program.

Example: 100 DATA 12, "Ralph", 01345, "NY"

This DATA statement holds four data items: 12, Ralph, 01345, and NY.

DCLEAR [DCL Shift E]

A command which closes and clears all open channels on a specific disk drive and device number. This is similar to OPEN 15,8,15,"IO":CLOSE15

Syntax: DCLEAR [Ddrive number] [<ON,>Udevice]

Example: DCLEAR D0

DCLOSE [D Shift C]

This command closes a single or all the files which are open on a disk drive.

Syntax: DCLOSE [#Logical file number] [<ON, >Udevice number]

Example: DCLOSE

DEC [none]

This numeric function calculates the decimal value of a hexadecimal string.

Example: PRINT DEC ("FF00")
          65280

DEF FN [64:D Shift E/128:none]

This is the Define Function. It lets you define special purpose formulas which will be used frequently within a BASIC program. The name of the function begins with FN and is followed by any alphanumeric name, beginning with a letter.

```
Syntax:   DEF FN name(variable) = expression

Example:  DEF FNC (X)=3.14159265*X^2
```

In this example, the name of the function is FNC. X is a dummy numeric variable. The expression after the equal sign is the formula for calculating the circumference of a circle.

DELETE [DE Shift L]

This command deletes lines from a BASIC program.

```
Syntax:   DELETE[First line][-Last line]

Example:  DELETE 10-70
```

This deletes lines 10 through 70.

DIM [D Shift I]

This dimension statement reserves memory space for array variables. It also defines an array as having one or more dimensions to it. All arrays having more than 11 items must be dimensioned with DIM.

```
Example:  DIM X(20)
```

This defines a one dimensional array named X to accommodate 21 items.

DIRECTORY [DI Shift R]

The F3 key on the C-128 is predefined to display the disk directory for drive 0, device 8. Any drive's directory can be viewed using this command.

Syntax: DIRECTORY [Ddrive number] [<ON, >Udevice number]
          [,Wildcard]

Example: DIRECTORY D1,U9

This displays the directory of drive 1, device 9.

DLOAD [D Shift L]

A command which loads a BASIC program from disk. Function key 2
activates DLOAD.

Syntax: DLOAD "Filename"[,Ddrive number] [,Udevice
          number]

Example: DLOAD "MEMO"   defaults to drive 0, device 8

DO/LOOP/WHILE/UNTIL/EXIT [none/LO Shift O/W Shift H/EX Shift I]

The DO/LOOP statement is a looping technique similar to FOR/NEXT.
All statements between the DO and the LOOP in a program are
continuously executed unless WHILE, UNTIL, or EXIT are encountered.

If EXIT is encountered, program execution passes to the statement
following the LOOP statement. If UNTIL is encountered, the program
loops until a condition is met. WHILE is the opposite of UNTIL: The
program continues while a certain condition is true. When the condition
becomes false, program execution passes to the statement following the
LOOP statement.

Example: 5 Y=15
          10 DO UNTIL Y=30
          15 Y=Y+1:PRINT Y
          20 LOOP
          30 PRINT "THIS LOOP ENDED WHEN Y BECAME 30."

DOPEN [D Shift O]

This command opens a disk file (sequential, relative, or random access)
for reading and/or writing.

Syntax: DOPEN#Logical file number, "Filename[,<S/P>]"
           [,Lrecord length][,Ddrive number][<ON, >Udevice
           number][,W]

S=Sequential file/P=Program file/L=Record length/W=Write operation.

Example: DOPEN#1, "CHECKS"

This opens a sequential file number 1, named Checks, for read access.

DRAW [D Shift R]

A graphics statement for drawing dots, lines, and other shapes on screen.

Syntax: DRAW[Color source] ,X1 ,Y1 [TO X2 ,Y2]...

Xl and Yl are starting coordinates from 0,0 to 320,200 and X2 and Y2
are ending coordinates.

Example: 60 DRAW 1, 120, 120 TO 300, 120

DS and DS$ [none/none]

System variables used for reading the disk drive command channel after
an error has occurred. DS returns the status of the drive's command
channel to find the cause of an error. DS$ defines the error in words.

Example: PRINT DS$

DSAVE [D Shift S]

This command saves a BASIC program onto disk. Function key 5
activates this command. The default device number is 8 and the default
drive number is 0.

Syntax: DSAVE "PROGRAM NAME" [,Ddrive number]
           [<ON, >Udevice number]

Example: DSAVE "MY PROGRAM"   this defaults to drive
           #0 and device#8

269

The example above could also be written as:
```
DSAVE "MY PROGRAM", D0, U8
```

DSAVE WITH REPLACE

If you want to resave an existing file that you just changed, you will need to DSAVE WITH REPLACE. Make sure that your disk has enough room for both the old and new versions of your file because both the old and new versions of the file are on the disk simultaneously at one point during the replace procedure.

```
Syntax:    DSAVE "@FILENAME" [,Ddrive#] [,Udevice#]

Example:   DSAVE "@MY PROGRAM"
```

DVERIFY [D Shift V]

This command checks a program on a specified disk drive against a program in memory.

```
Syntax:    DVERIFY "FILENAME"[ ,Ddrive number][<ON,>Udevice
           number]

Example:   DVERIFY "My Program"
```

This verifies My Program on drive 0, unit 8.

EL [none]

This system variable is used for error trapping. EL identifies the line in which an error has occurred.

END [64:E Shift N/128:none]

This statement stops a program's execution and returns the computer to immediate mode.

ENVELOPE [E Shift N]

This statement is used to define a musical instrument by setting the envelope number(N), attack rate(A), decay rate(D), sustain(S), release(R), waveform(WF), and pulse width(]PW).

Syntax: ENVELOPE N[,A][,D] [,S] [,R] [,WF][,PW]

N=0-9/A=0-15/D=0-15/S=0-15/R=0-15/WF:0=triangle; 1=sawtooth; 2=variable pulse(square); 3=noise; 4=ring modulation/PW=0-4095.

ER [none]

A system variable used in error trapping which holds the definition of the most recent error encountered.

ERR$ [E Shift R]

This function is used for reading an error message from an error encountered in a BASIC program.

Example: PRINT ERR$(ER)

EXIT (see DO/LOOP/WHILE/UNTIL/EXIT)

EXP [E Shift X]

This numeric function calculates the mathematical constant e (2.7182813) to an indicated power of N.

Syntax: EXP(N)

FAST [none]

This command puts the C-128 into 2 MHz mode of operation for speedy I/O operations. This turns off the 40-column screen until the SLOW command is given.

FETCH [F Shift E]

This statement is used for getting data from the RAM expansion module on the C-128.

Syntax: FETCH #Bytes,Start of Host RAM, Expansion Bank, Start of Expansion RAM.

FILTER [F Shift I]

A music statement for programming the SID chip's various filters.

Syntax: FILTER [Frequency] [,Low Pass] [,Bank Pass] [,High Pass] [,Resonance]

FOR/TO/STEP/NEXT [F Shift O/none/ST Shift E/N Shift E]

A looping statement structure which is used to count the number of times that a portion of a BASIC program is executed.

Example: 10 FOR T= 1 TO 100 STEP 5
            20 PRINT T
            30 NEXT T

FRE [F Shift R]

This numeric function computes the number of free bytes available for BASIC programs (N=0) and for BASIC variable storage (N=1).

Example: PRINT FRE(0)

GET [G Shift E]

A programming statement which sends one character at a time from the keyboard to memory whenever a key is pressed. If a key is not pressed, then the program will continue execution automatically.

Example: 10 GET X$:IF X$ = " " THEN 10

GETKEY [GETK Shift E]

This statement receives input data from the keyboard one character at a time. It waits for the user to type a character before letting the program continue execution.

Example: 10 GETKEY N$

GET# [none]

This statement requests data, one character at a time, from a tape, disk, or the RS232 port. A file has to have been opened.

Example: 10 GET#15, N$

GO [none]

This dummy statement is always used with TO. GO TO is usually combined into a one word statement: GOTO. See GOTO.

GO64 [none]

The command used for accessing 64 mode from 128 mode on the C-128.

Example: GO64 <RETURN>
            Are you sure?

GOSUB/RETURN [GO Shift S/RE Shift T]

This statement calls a subroutine for execution that appears in another location within a BASIC program. Once the subroutine has been completed, program execution returns to the line after the GOSUB.

Example: 10 GOSUB 300
            20 PRINT "THIS IS WHERE THE PROGRAM CONTINUES
            AFTER THE GOSUB ROUTINE HAS FINISHED"
            30 ...
            40 ...
            300 PRINT "HERE IS THE SUBROUTINE. " :RETURN

273

GOTO [G Shift O]

This statement transfers program execution to the line number specified.

Example: 10 IF X=1 THEN GOTO 50

GRAPHIC [G Shift R]

This statement puts the C-128 into one of six graphics modes.

Syntax: GRAPHIC Mode[,Clear][,S] or GRAPHIC CLR

The six graphics modes are:
    0=40 column text
    1=standard bit mapped
    2=standard bit mapped split screen
    3=multicolor bit mapped
    4=multicolor bit mapped split screen
    5=80 column text.

Example: 10 GRAPHIC 1,1

This activates the standard bit-mapped graphics mode and clears the screen.

GSHAPE   (See SSHAPE).

HEADER [HE Shift A]

This command is for formatting a disk.

Syntax: HEADER "DISKNAME"[,Ii.d.number] [,Ddrive number]
          [<ON,>Udevice number]

Example: HEADER "THISDISK",I22,D0

This formats a disk, named THISDISK, with a disk i.d. number of 22, on Drive 0 (for a single disk drive). The device defaults to 8.

HELP [none]

This command is available for use when a BASIC programming error has occurred. HELP will list the erred line and highlight the line segment where the error happened.

HEX$ [H Shift E]

This function displays a four character hexadecimal number from a decimal number.

Syntax: HEX$ (N)

Example: PRINT HEX$ (65)
           0041

IF/THEN/ELSE [none/none/none]

This statement evaluates a BASIC expression and takes one of two actions. When the IF expression is true, the THEN statement is executed. When the IF expression is false, then program execution falls to the next line number, unless an ELSE clause is present. When an ELSE clause is present on the same line as the IF/THEN, it is executed when the IF expression is false.

Syntax: IF <expression> THEN <statement>:[ELSE clause]

Example: 5 INPUT Y
           10 IF Y=5 THEN GOTO 20:ELSE GOTO 5
           20 PRINT "Y IS 5."

INPUT [none]

This statement asks the user to type in specific information. The program displays a question mark on screen, waits for the user to enter a response, and press the Return key.

Example: 5 INPUT "GUESS A NUMBER BETWEEN 1 AND 10.";N
           10 IF N=3 THEN PRINT "YOU GUESSED IT!":GOTO 20
           15 PRINT " NO. TRY AGAIN.":GOTO 5
           20 END

275

INPUT# [I Shift N]

This INPUT statement gets its information from a disk or tape file rather than from the user. The information is then used in a BASIC program.

```
Example:   5 OPEN 15, 8, 15
          10 FOR T=1 TO 25
          20 INPUT #15, A$, X, B$
          30 NEXT T
          40 CLOSE 15
```

INSTR [IN Shift S]

This function will search for the location of a string within another string and display the numeric value of its starting position.

```
Example:   PRINT INSTR ("WHERE IS IT?", "IS")
          7
```

INT [none]

This numeric function converts a numeric expression to the nearest whole number which is less than or equal to the expression. INT displays the integer value.

```
Example:   PRINT INT(2. 156)
          2
```

JOY [J Shift O]

This function displays the position of a joystick and the status of the fire button.

```
Syntax:    JOY (N)
```

N is 1 or 2. Any value of 128 or more means that the fire button is also pressed.

```
Example:   PRINT JOY (2)
          128
```

This shows that the joystick in port 2 had its fire button depressed.

KEY [K Shift E]

This statement is used to define the purposes of the eight function keys.

Syntax: KEY [key number, string]

Example: KEY 1, "OPEN4, 4:CMD4:LIST" + CHR$ (13)

This defines F1 to list the current BASIC program in memory to the printer.

LEFT$ [LE Shift E]

LEFT String is a function which returns a specified number of the leftmost characters of a string.

Example: 10 X$="WHAT IS IT?"
           20 PRINT LEFT$ (X$, 4)
           RUN
           WHAT

LEN [none]

This function determines the length of a string.

Example: X$="RUN MAGAZINE"
           PRINT LEN (X$)
           12

LET [L Shift E]

This is an optional statement used for defining a variable.

Example: LET X=100
This could be written X=100.

LIST [L Shift I]

This command will display on the screen all of the statements in a BASIC program, or those specified by the user.

Syntax: LIST [First line] [-Last line]

Example: LIST 10-40

LOAD [L Shift O]

This command is used for loading programs from either tape or disk.

Syntax: LOAD "PROGRAM" [,Device number] [,Relocate
           flag]

Examples: LOAD "DISK PROGRAM", 8
          LOAD "TAPE PROGRAM"

LOCATE X,Y [LO Shift C]

A graphics command which lets the user place the pixel cursor anywhere on a high resolution screen. X and Y coordinates can range from 0,0 to 320,200.

Example: LOCATE 100, 100

LOG [none]

This function returns the natural logarithm of a positive number.

Syntax: LOG(X)

LOOP (See DO/LOOP/WHILE/UNTIL/EXIT)

MID$ [M Shift I]

MID String is a function which locates a substring within a larger string by specifying its starting position and its length.

Example: X$="RUN IT RIGHT"
           PRINT MID$(X$, 5, 2)
           IT

MONITOR [MO Shift N]

This command is used for entering the built-in machine language monitor of the C-l28.

```
Syntax:    MONITOR
```

MOVSPR [M Shift O]

A statement used for positioning or moving a sprite on screen.

```
Example:  MOVSPR 1, 100, 100
```

This will position sprite # 1 at screen location 100,100.

NEW [none]

This command erases a BASIC program from memory and clears all variables.

NEXT (See FOR/TO/STEP/NEXT)

ON [none]

This conditional statement is used with GOTO and GOSUB to branch to a specified line number when a certain condition is met. ON allows program execution to branch to the line numbers listed, depending upon the value of the expression following ON. If the expression is valued at 1, then the program branches to the first line number; if the expression is 2, then the program branches to the second line number; and so forth. ON-GOTO/GOSUB is actually a method for using several IF-conditions in one program line.

```
Example:   10  INPUT K$
           20  ON K$ GOSUB 100, 200, 300, 400
```

OPEN [O Shift P]

This statement is used for opening a disk, tape, printer, or screen for file input or output.

Example: OPEN 15, 8, 15

The logical file number is 15, the device number is 8 (disk drive), and the secondary address is 15.

OR [none]

A logical operator that calculates conditions as true or false.

PAINT [P Shift A]

A graphics statement used for filling an area with a specified color.

Syntax: PAINT[Color Source] , X, Y[, Mode]

(See RCLR for discussion of Color Source.)
Modes: 0=defined by color source/1=defined by non-background source)
X,Y is the starting coordinate from 0,0 to 320,200.

Example: 70 PAINT 1, 149, 101, 0

This will fill in a circular shape built with the examples from BOX, CHAR, CIRCLE, COLOR, DRAW, and GRAPHIC in this glossary.

PEEK [64:P Shift E/128:PE Shift E]

This numeric function returns the contents of a specified memory location, returning a result between 0 and 255.

Example: PRINT PEEK(53280)
            253

PEN [P Shift E]

This function reveals the coordinates of a light pen.

PI [pi symbol]

This variable returns the value of pi.
(3.14159265).

PLAY [P Shift L]

This musical statement lets you select the voice, octave, envelope, volume, and the notes that you want played within a BASIC program.

```
Syntax:   PLAY "Voice, Octave, Tune Envelope, Volume,
          Filter, Elements"
```

POINTER

This function is used for finding the address of a specific variable.

```
Example:  X=POINTER( Y)
```

POKE [64:P Shift O/128:PO Shift O]

This statement changes the value of any memory location in RAM.

```
Example:  POKE 53280, 1
```
This changes the VIC border color.

POS [none]

This function is used for finding the current cursor column position within a defined window.

```
Example:  PRINT POS (X)
```

POT [P Shift O]

This function can tell both the direction of a game paddle and whether the fire button has been pressed.

```
Example:  PRINT POT (N)
```

PRINT [?]

A commonly used statement which outputs words and numbers to the screen.

Example: PRINT "THIS IS THE SPECIAL ISSUE."
THIS IS THE SPECIAL ISSUE.

PRINT# [P Shift R]

This statement outputs information to peripherals such as printers, disk drives, and cassette players.

Example: OPEN4, 4: CMD4
PRINT#4, "Here it is"
CLOSE4

PRINT USING [? US Shift I]

This statement defines the format of words and numbers for printing to the screen, printer, or other device.

Syntax: PRINT [#Filenumber] USING "format list";print list

PUDEF [P Shift UE]

This statement allows redefinition of any of four symbols used in a PRINT USING statement (in the following order): blanks, commas, decimal points, and dollar signs.

Syntax: PUDEF "nnnn"

Example: PUDEF "*"

This places an asterisk where any blank occurs.

RCLR [R Shift C]

This function gives the specific color of any requested color source.

Syntax: RCLR (X)

X is the color source 0-6. The color source numbers are as follows:
0   40-column background
1   bit mapped foreground

2   multicolor 1
3   multicolor 2
4   40-column border
5   40/80 column characters
6   80-column background

Example: PRINT RCLR(0)

This would print the color (1-16) of a background in 40-column mode.

RDOT [R Shift D]

This function is used to locate a pixel cursor on a high resolution screen and to tell its color.

Syntax: RDOT(N)

0=X coordinate, 1=Y coordinate, 2=color source

Examples: PRINT RDOT (0)   returns X coordinate position
          of pixel cursor
          PRINT RDOT (1)   returns Y coordinate position
          of pixel cursor
          PRINT RDOT (2)   returns color source of pixel
          cursor

READ [64:R Shift E/128:RE Shift A]

This statement Reads the numbers and text held within Data statements in a BASIC program.

Example: 5 READ X
          10 PRINT X
          15 IF X=5 THEN END
          20 GOTO 5
          30 DATA 1, 2, 3, 4, 5
          40 END

This program reads data from line 30 (1,2,3,4,5) and prints each number. The program continues to read and print each number until the program reaches the data number 5 and prints that number. At that point, the program ends.

RECORD [R Shift E]

This is used with relative files. It positions a relative file pointer at any specified byte of data within a record for reading or writing data.

Syntax: RECORD#Logical file number,Record number[,Byte number]

Example: RECORD#2, 22,4

REM [none]

This statement is used for personal commentary about a BASIC program within that program. All REM statements are ignored by the computer and are never executed.

Example: 10 REM PROGRAM WRITTEN BY MARY DOE

RENAME [RE Shift N]

This command is used for changing the name of a file on disk.

Syntax: RENAME "Old name" TO "New name"[,Ddrive number] [,Udevice number]

RENUMBER [REN Shift U]

This command renumbers the lines of a BASIC program.

Syntax: RENUMBER [New start][,increment][,Old line]

RESTORE [RE Shift S]

This statement resets the READ pointer so that previously read data can be read again.

Syntax: RESTORE [line number]

Example: RESTORE 100

This resets the pointer to line 100 where old DATA statements will be re-read.

RESUME [RES Shift U]

This is an aid to programmers when an error has been encountered within a BASIC program. This statement tells the computer where to continue program execution after an error has been trapped. With no parameter, it tries to again execute the line with the error. With a line number, it will GOTO the specified line to resume execution. With NEXT, it resumes execution at the statement immediately after the one with the error.

```
Syntax:    RESUME [Line number/NEXT]

Example:   RESUME 10
```

RETURN [RE Shift T]

This is used with a GOSUB statement and returns program execution to the next statement after the occurance of the GOSUB.

```
Example:   10 GOSUB 500: PRINT "BACK AGAIN?"
           20 ...
           500 INPUT "PRESS ANY KEY TO CONTINUE";X$;RETURN
```

RGR [R Shift G]

This function returns the current graphics mode of the computer. X is a dummy argument that you specify. The value returned by RGR(X) refers to these modes:

Graphics Mode	Value
40 column (VIC) text	0
Standard bit map	1
Split screen bit map	2
Multicolor bit map	3
Split screen multicolor bit map	4
80 column text	5

```
Syntax:    RGR(X)

Example:   PRINT RGR(0)
           1
```

In this example, the current graphic mode is returned as 1, which is standard bit map mode.

RIGHT$ [R Shift I]

This string function returns the rightmost characters from a string of text.

```
Example:   X$="SPECIAL ISSUE"
           PRINT RIGHT$(X$, 3)
           SUE
```

RND [R Shift N]

A function used to generate a random number between 0 and 1.

```
Example:   X=INT (RND(1)*5)+1
```

X will be a whole number between 1 and 5.

RSPCOLOR [RSP Shift C]

This function returns the color values of a multicolored sprite.

```
Syntax:    RSPCOLOR (X)
```

X is Register number (1 or 2). When X=1, RSPCOLOR returns the sprite multicolor 1. When X=2, this function returns the sprite multicolor 2. The returned color values range from 1 to 16.

RSPPOS [R Shift S]

This function returns the speed and position of a sprite.

```
Syntax:    RSPPOS Sprite#,Position/Speed
```

RSPRITE [RSP Shift R]

This function returns the six characteristics of a sprite. These characteristics will have been previously specified in the SPRITE command.

```
Example:   5 FOR X=1 TO 6
          10 PRINT RSPRITE (1,X)
          20 NEXT X
```

RUN [R Shift U]

This command executes a BASIC program in memory. RUN can be used with a line number to begin execution at that line. It can also be used to load and execute a BASIC program from disk.

```
Syntax:   RUN    (after you load a program into memory)
          RUN [Line number]
          RUN "Filename" [ ,Ddrive number] [,Udevice
          number]
```

```
Example:  RUN "MY PROGRAM"
```

RWINDOW [R Shift W]

This function returns the size of a screen window. The number of lines (0), rows (1), and whether the display is 40 or 80 columns (2) are returned.

```
Syntax:RWINDOW (X)
```

where X is 0, 1, or 2.

SAVE [S Shift A]

A command used for storing programs on disk or tape. Without a specified file name, SAVE automatically tries to store the program to tape.

```
Syntax:   SAVE ["Filename"] [ ,device number] [ ,EOT flag]
```

Device number of 1 is tape; 8 is a disk drive. If EOT is 1, then the end of tape flag is set.

```
Example:  SAVE "MY PROGRAM",8        saves to disk
          SAVE "MY PROGRAM"          saves to tape
```

SCALE [SC Shift A]

This statement changes the scaling of bit mapped images in multicolor and high resolution modes.

Syntax: SCALE N[, X max, Y max]

Example: SCALE 1   turns on scaling.
            SCALE 0   turns off scaling.

SCNCLR [S Shift C]

This statement clears the screen in the graphics mode specified.

Syntax: SCNCLR Mode # (0-5)

SCRATCH [SC Shift R]

This disk command erases a file from disk and deletes its reference from the disk directory.

Syntax: SCRATCH "Filename" [,Ddrive number] [,Udevice number]

Example: SCRATCH "RUNFILE", D1

This deletes the file RUNFILE from the disk in drive #1 in a dual disk drive system.

SGN [S Shift G]

This function returns the sign (positive, negative, or zero) of a number.

Example: PRINT SGN(X)

SIN [S Shift I]

This function identifies the sine of a number measured in radians.

Example: PRINT SIN(X)

SLEEP [S Shift L]

This statement delays program execution for a specified number of seconds (0 to 65535).

Syntax: SLEEP N

SLOW [none]

This statement returns the computer to 1 MHz speed of operation after the FAST command.

SOUND [S Shift O]

This statement is used for creating sounds and music on the C-128. Seven parameters can be defined with this statement.

Syntax: SOUND V, F, D[, DIR] [, M] [, S] [, W] [, P]

V=voice, F=frequency, D=duration, DIR=stop direction, M=minimum frequency, S=step value, W=waveform, P=pulse width.

SPC [64:S Shift P/128:none]

This function is used for spacing of characters within PRINT and PRINT# statements.

Example: PRINT "HI"; SPC (10) ; "THERE"
            HI   THERE

(10 spaces separate HI and THERE)

SPRCOLOR [SPR Shift C]

This statement is used for setting multicolor 1 and/or 2 for sprites.

Example: SPRCOLOR 5, 6

This sets multicolor 1 to purple and multicolor 2 to green for all sprites within a BASIC program.

289

SPRDEF [SPR Shift D]

This command is used to enter the built-in sprite editor of the C-128.

SPRITE [S Shift P]

This statement activates and deactivates sprites' colors, it expands sprites, and it sets the screen priorities for any of eight sprites.

Syntax: SPRITE <#>[, On(1)/Off(0)][, Foreground color (1-16)][, Priority (0-in front of screen objects/1-in back of)][, Horizontal expansion (1-on/0-off)] [, Vertical expansion (1-on/0-off)] [, Mode (0-standard/1-multicolor)]

Example: SPRITE 2,1,8,0,0,1,0

SPRSAV [SPR Shift S]

This statement transfers 63 bytes of sprite data from a text string variable into a storage area in memory. A sprite image can be stored as a string variable; the data within a string variable can be transferred into a sprite; and one sprite's data can be duplicated in a second sprite.

Syntax: SPRSAV<Origin> , <Destination>

SQR [S Shift Q]

This function returns the square root of a number.

Example: X=81
          PRINT SQR (X)
          9

SSHAPE/GSHAPE [S Shift S/G Shift S]

These two statements are used for saving and loading rectangular areas of high resolution/multicolor screens to and from BASIC string variables. After you have drawn a figure on screen, you use SSHAPE to save its bit mapped image and location. Use GSHAPE to retrieve the data.

Syntax: SSHAPE string variable, X1,Y1 corner
         coordinates[,X2,Y2 opposite corner coordinates]

Syntax: GSHAPE string variable [X,Y corner coordinates]
         [,Replacement mode (0-place as was saved, 1-
         invert shape, 2-OR shape with the area, 3- AND
         shape with the area, 4- XOR shape]

ST [none]

This system variable defines the status of the system after an input/output
operation has occurred.

STASH [S Shift T]

This statement is used with the RAM memory expander. It moves the
contents of memory into the expansion RAM.

STEP   (See FOR/TO/NEXT/STEP)

STOP [64:S Shift T/128:ST Shift O]

This statement stops execution of a BASIC program and displays a
BREAK message on screen identifying the line number where the stop
occurred.

Example: 10 X=X+1
          20 PRINT X
          30 IF X=25 THEN STOP
          40 GOTO 10

STR$ [ST Shift R]

This string function converts a number into a string so that the number
can be used with text string functions.

Example: 5 X=225. 1
          10 PRINT "$";STR$ (X) + "0"

This will display the number X as $225.10 rather than as $225.1

291

SWAP [S Shift W]

This statement is used with the RAM memory expander. It swaps the contents of the computer's internal RAM with the contents of the external RAM expander.

Syntax: SWAP #Bytes, Starting address of host RAM (0-65535), 64K RAM expansion bank # (0-3), Starting address of RAM expansion (0-65535).

SYS [S Shift Y]

This statement calls and executes a machine language subroutine from within a BASIC program or from immediate mode.

Syntax: SYS Address
or   SYS Address [,A][,X][,Y][,S]

A is accumulator; X, Y, and Status are registers.

TAB [T Shift A]

A statement used in PRINT and PRINT# statements for placing an expression at a specific horizontal position on screen.

Example: PRINT TAB(5);"THESE WORDS ARE INDENTED FIVE SPACES"

TAN [none]

This numeric function identifies the tangent of an angle in radians.

Example: PRINT TAN(X)

TEMPO [T Shift E]

A musical statement which defines the speed of a song to be played.

Syntax: TEMPO X   where X is 0-255.

TI and TI$ [none/none]

These are system variables used for reading the 24 hour real time clock built into the computer. TI is the current numeric value of the clock in 1/60th seconds. TI$ is the string that reads TI as a 24 hour clock.

Example: TI$="121005"

This is 12:10 pm and 5 seconds.

TO (See FOR/TO/STEP/NEXT)

TRAP [T Shift R]

This statement is an error detector within a running BASIC program. When a bug is discovered, program execution is transferred to a prespecified line number. The EL variable will identify the line in which the error occurred; ER will specify the error condition; and ERR$ will actually display the error message.

Syntax: TRAP [line #]

Example: 100 TRAP 200

if an error occurs, go to line 200

        200 PRINT ERR$ (ER);EL

print error message and the error line number

        210 RESUME

resume with program execution

TROFF [TRO Shift F]

This statement turns off tracing mode.

TRON [TR Shift O]

This statement turns on tracing mode for use when debugging BASIC programs. When activated and a program is running, the line numbers of the program are displayed before each line is executed so that the programmer can easily see where an error occurs.

UNTIL (See DO/LOOP/WHILE/UNTIL/EXIT)

USR [U Shift S]

This function transfers program execution from BASIC to a machine language program. Variables can be passed between BASIC and ML using this function.

VAL [none]

This function translates a string holding numbers into a number. It specifies the numeric value of the string by searching for numbers from left to right. Upon encountering an invalid character, it halts.

```
Example:   X$="15 MILES"
           PRINT VAL(X$)
           15
```

VERIFY [V Shift E]

This command verifies that a program in memory is the same program as the one on disk or tape. This is a safety feature which lets you ensure that the program you saved has really been saved in its entirety. For tape users, VERIFY is used for determining the free space on tape for the next program to be saved.

```
Syntax:    VERIFY "PROGRAM NAME"[,Device number][,Relocate
           flag (0 loads to the start of BASIC/1 loads to
           where the program was originally saved from)]
```

VOL [V Shift O]

A musical statement which defines the volume of sounds produced with the SOUND and PLAY statements. Volume can be set from 0 to 15.

WAIT [W Shift O]

This statement pauses program execution while the computer monitors the status of the Input/Output registers searching for a particular value. WAIT is used when performing certain I/O operations.

Syntax: WAIT<Location>,<Mask 1>[,<Mask 2>]

WHILE (See DO/LOOP/WHILE/UNTIL/EXIT)

WIDTH [WI Shift D]

This statement determines the width of the pixel cursor used for drawing lines with the graphic commands.

Syntax: WIDTH 1   sets a single width.
           WIDTH 2   sets a double width.

WINDOW [W Shift I]

This statement is used for identifying a screen window in 40 or 80 column text mode. Coordinates range from 0-39/0-79 horizontally and 0-24 vertically.

Syntax: WINDOW Top left column, Top left row, Bottom
           right column, Bottom right row [,Clear (1 to
           clear the window)]

Example: WINDOW 50,10,70,20,1

This defines and clears a window whose top left point is 50,10 and whose bottom right point is 70,20.

XOR [X Shift O]

A function which provides the exclusive OR of two specified argument values.

```
Syntax:   XOR (X1, X2)
```

Xl and X2 range from 0-65535.

Appendix F

C-128 Five Configurations

This is the default startup mode. Disk drive off. Turn on the power switch and 128 mode boots up. After boot up, turn on your disk drive.

1. 128 Mode: 40 columns

Keep the 40/80 key raised. Composite monitor, or TV. If using the 1902 monitor, set it for "separated chroma/luma" before turning on the computer.

2. 128 Mode: 80 columns

Depress the 40/80 key. RGBI monitor. If using the 1902, set it for "RGBI" before turning on the computer.

You can switch between 40 and 80 columns by pressing ESC and then pressing X. Then, switch to your other monitor or reset the 1902 to the other display. Or, you could reboot. Make sure to save your work since changing operating modes erases memory.

64 MODE

3. 64 Mode: 40 columns only

Composite monitor or T.V.
   a. From 128 mode, type GO 64 and answer "Y" to enter 64 mode.
   b. Or, before powering up, hold down the Commodore key and turn on the power switch to   startup in 64 mode.
   c. Or, before powering up, insert a C-64 software cartridge and then turn on the power switch.

To exit 64 mode, turn off the computer. If you have a cartridge inserted, turn off the computer and then remove the cartridge before trying to enter any of the other modes.

Turn on your disk drive. Place the CP/M System Disk into your disk drive. Turn on the power switch.

4. CP/M Mode: 40 columns

Keep the 40/80 key raised. Composite monitor, or TV. If using the 1902 monitor, set it for "separated chroma/luma" before powering up.

5. CP/M Mode: 80 columns

Depress the 40/80 key. RGBI monitor. If using the 1902, set it for "RGBI" before powering up.

To enter CP/M mode from 128 mode: select your preferred screen width. Type BOOT and Return.

To enter CP/M mode from 64 mode: Turn off your computer. Select your preferred screen width, as outlined above. Turn on your disk drive. Insert the CP/M System Disk into your disk drive. Turn on the computer.

To change between 40 and 80, turn off your computer and change the 40/80 key. Switch to your other monitor or reset the 1902. Turn on the computer. If you are in 40 columns, you can keep the computer on, switch to your other monitor or reset the 1902 to 80 columns, and press the Reset switch.

www.ingramcontent.com/pod-product-compliance
Lightning Source LLC
Chambersburg PA
CBHW071407050326

40689CB00010B/1782